C000181388

Language Development for Maths

Circle Time Sessions to Improve Communication Skills in Maths

Marion Nash and Jackie Lowe

 David Fulton Publishers

David Fulton Publishers Ltd
The Chiswick Centre, 414 Chiswick High Road, London W4 5TF

www.fultonpublishers.co.uk

First published in Great Britain in 2004 by David Fulton Publishers

10 9 8 7 6 5 4 3 2 1

Note: The right of the individual contributors to be identified as the authors of their work has been asserted by them in accordance with the Copyright, Designs and Patents Act 1988.

Copyright © Marion Nash and Jackie Lowe 2004

British Library Cataloguing in Publication Data
A catalogue record for this book is available from the British Library

David Fulton Publishers is a division of Granada Learning, part of ITV plc.

ISBN 1–84312–171–9

All rights reserved. The material in this publication may be photocopied for use within the purchasing organisation. Otherwise, no part of this publication may be reproduced, stored in a retrieval system or transmitted, in any form, or by any means, electronic, mechanical, photocopying, recording or otherwise, without the prior permission of the publishers.

Typeset by FiSH Books, London
Printed and bound in Great Britain

Contents

To my partner David, with love
Thank you for your wonderful enthusiasm and technical support.

(Marion Nash)

Acknowledgements

The publication of this book has been made possible by the foresight and support of the people who work in the Plymouth Education Authority and those who direct it. The work has been supported and encouraged by Bronwen Lacy, Director for Lifelong Learning and Maggie Carter, Head of Service (Learner Support), in line with their commitment to enrich the educational experiences of children in the City of Plymouth. As a result, many children in other areas will also have the opportunity to grow in confidence and develop new skills through working with the materials.

Ford Primary School in Plymouth is at the heart of the development of the Spirals programme, and this book. Many thanks to the Head, staff (in particular Val Galer who continues the important work of running the groups); also governors and parents. Thanks particularly to the children who were the initial inspiration for the work. Highfield Primary School in Plymouth has played an increasingly important role in supporting the development of Spirals. Many thanks to Paddy Marsh, the Head; Linda Mercer, the SENCO; and the staff, parents and children. I have also found a great deal of interest in and inspiration from the ideas of Jenny Mosley, Ann Locke and Ruth Durch (Brightstart).

Special thanks to Linda Evans (Fultons) for her interest, enthusiasm, and guidance. Many thanks to Jenny and Geoff who made the accompanying video material. Their professionalism, patience and good humour made working with them great fun.

Thanks to the Plymouth Educational Psychology team and in particular Mick Johnson for his much appreciated support and enthusiasm for the Spirals work. Special thanks to the admin team especially Sally and Liz.

Many thanks to my partner David, whose creative formatting skills and warm support have been invaluable, also to my family and especially my grandson Tom who provided the original inspiration for this series of books.

This book contains many traditional tried and tested materials and if I have omitted to attribute material to anybody it is not intentional and I hereby take this opportunity to thank them.

The Mr Badger Map (p. 156) has been reprinted by kind permission of Black Sheep Press.

Marion Nash, Educational Psychologist

Video CD and training

There is a 30-minute video recorded on to a CD contained in this pack. This features Educational Psychologist Marion Nash and Speech and Language Therapist Jackie Lowe, describing the Spirals programme. There are also extracts from a Spirals session run by Marion, SENCO Linda Mercer and teacher Carole Penton at Highfield Primary School in Plymouth, demonstrating the small group Circle Time approach. This will be a useful resource for schools preparing to use the Spirals materials and is easily accessed via the CD drive in your computer.

Marion Nash has teamed up with Granada Learning Professional Development to offer a training package to LEAs and clusters of schools considering adopting the Spirals programme. You can obtain more information about this by telephoning Alastair Durno on 020 8996 6032.

The video CD has been made by Jeff Booth of Highfield Productions (Tel. 01548 830274).

Introduction

Spirals Maths came about largely because of the success of our initial language development programme (*Language Development: Circle Time Sessions to Improve Communication Skills*: see page 140 for details). The programme is based on the Circle Time ethos, which has been widely promoted by Leslie Button, Jenny Mosley and others in recent years. In 2000/2001, I worked alongside Jackie Lowe, a senior Speech and Language Therapist, and teacher Tracey Palmer, to plan a series of carefully crafted sessions to develop language skills and thinking skills in linguistically vulnerable children. Before long, schools trialing the sessions were reporting pleasing gains made by the children involved. Teachers were observing gains made on several fronts:

- listening and concentration skills;
- expressive and receptive language;
- confidence and self-esteem.

These gains were also seen to transfer to the large group/classroom situation and evidence is now emerging of a positive effect on progress in reading as well.

This success is undoubtedly due, at least in part, to the supportive Circle Time ethos as applied to the small group sessions. These are all planned to incorporate:

- movement for a purpose;
- talking and questioning;
- music, rhythm and rhyme;
- critical reasoning and thinking;
- social skills;
- emotional awareness.

Teachers and Speech and Language Therapists were pleased with the successes they were experiencing in supporting children through Spirals groups and began asking us to develop a similar scheme with Maths vocabulary in mind.

We took on the task enthusiastically and looked at establishing a course which would develop familiarity with Maths-related words, and correct and confident use of this vocabulary. Activities were built in to create an understanding that words can have dual meanings and that the context must be looked at to provide clues about what is meant; for example, 'more' – we can give a child a large glass of milk. When they ask for **more** we put more milk into the glass but it may be a smaller amount than the original. It is less but it's still more! There are many anomalies to be found in mathematical language and this may be one of the underlying reasons why children struggle.

One answer is to plan ways of presenting mathematical concepts at the right level and in different ways, which will engage all learning styles and help learners to bring all their strengths to bear on the task. Use of Spirals groups built around this system will enable a wide range of children to experience success in early Maths.

Parents and carers are key partners in the learning process for the child, and have responded enthusiastically to our Home Activities work books which accompany and support the Spirals language sessions, so naturally we have devised a second Home book to accompany the Spirals Maths sessions. This outlines simple activities for supporting the work going on in school in a fun and stress-free way (details are on page 140).

Language and Maths

The language of Maths can be confusing to the child. Furthermore, extended verbal explanations can actually create barriers to understanding which are difficult for the child to overcome.

A fast pace in the learning environment can exacerbate this effect and leave children convinced that they do not have the skills to achieve in Maths. Children may then become stressed by their own lack of understanding and experience a range of negative emotions: embarrassment, fear, anger and further confusion, and an overwhelming urge to escape from the learning situation which they see as the cause of their unease.

The children may or may not have needs which require special educational support, but they do need special help to overcome the confidence barrier and negative emotions before they can engage productively with the learning process and experience success.

This is where the Circle Time ethos can help by providing a secure and highly motivating teaching and learning environment which addresses personal confidence needs and lowers tension. Spirals group work adds to this a slower pace and conscious strategies to engage effective thinking. Spirals work encourages children to develop and use a range of skills to bring to a wide range of tasks.

In Spirals groups we are not seeking to teach skills and concepts directly. We provide a learning atmosphere in which children are enabled to discover that such things exist. They are then motivated through the fun activities in the group to engage in learning and mastering these skills and concepts in order to be able to enter into playing the games successfully. This new-found confidence in learning will normally transfer into the classroom.

Through these Spirals Maths sessions we raise awareness of concepts such as time, shape, length, measurement, weight, pattern formation and other key concepts, and begin to familiarise children with Maths-linked vocabulary. The sessions also help the children to begin to develop problem-solving and thinking strategies. As children progress, the adult can pop in questions to orient the children to think about the skills they are using to solve problems, thus creating a powerful tool for learning.

What happens in the group

In a small group, we are able to be sensitive to the different learning and teaching styles of the children and the staff involved. Each session is crafted to provide a range of learning inputs.

- Each session is based on activities to promote reflection and critical thinking.
- The supportive principles of Circle Time are drawn upon to provide a group ethos in which we can foster the children's confidence in putting ideas forward. The sessions highlight the importance of 'brainstorming'; that is, allowing everyone to bring their ideas to a task before we select (but not judge) the most appropriate answer.
- The levels of activity and focus are carefully balanced to achieve motivation and optimum attention. The pace and language is deliberately slowed down. This has a tremendously positive impact on behaviour as children realise they can access the activities fully.
- The content of the sessions includes number work and mathematical concepts, but also thinking skills, prediction, reasoning, hypothesis development and checking, and effective questioning.
- The sessions give opportunities for dynamic assessment of children's needs and progress which can be supplemented in class lessons.
- Listening and turn-taking are an integral part of the course.
- Visualisation and harnessing imagination are introduced as powerful learning tools.
- Speaking with confidence and clarity to an audience and communicating their thinking is an outcome which is carefully planned for.

The course as a whole prepares children for the transition from learning from experience to learning from direct teaching by encouraging their ability to listen, to visualise an action, number or quantity, and to recall and describe events.

What are the effects of the group on the children?

The children become much more skilled and effective thinkers and communicators. The group allows them to overcome the barriers to learning and to bring their 'heart, mind and hand' to the task. Learning is fun and relaxed, and therefore memorable and likely to endure and develop over time.

Children are highly motivated through the fun feeling to the group. They find they are concentrating almost without realising it, and contributing answers and ideas – perhaps for the first time since starting school.

In the small group we are able to keep the instructional language straightforward and not too demanding. The children blossom as they find that they can more easily understand the language, and slowly gain confidence in learning and talking in more formal situations.

Teachers often report that after only four sessions they see positive changes in children's attitudes and behaviour.

How to use this book

Who are the intended group?

- The course contained in this book has been developed to aid linguistically challenged children; children who find it difficult to understand verbal instructions and who do not have the skills or confidence to frame questions to clarify their understanding, or to speak out in a large group.
- The content relates to the language skills required to develop understanding of basic mathematical concepts.
- The activities are designed to achieve a balance of movement and focus, to maintain concentration and to help achieve mastery – a range of concepts, skills and processes are developed through the games.
- Over and above this, the children develop confidence in themselves as learners – this confidence carries over to other situations including the classroom.

Before running the groups

1 Involve staff in discussion about the aims of the group and children who would benefit from inclusion in the group.
2 Involve parents and carers. Seek parental permission if an outside agency is involved in running the group with the school.
3 Assess: (a) take a snapshot of the children's strengths and difficulties with the individual assessment form provided on page 8, using one copy for each pupil; (b) plan targets for the group. Individual IEPs may be used where appropriate.
4 Identify two people who will be running the group. This is a necessity, not a luxury.
5 Create a box of resources to keep on hand for the group. Some materials are provided in the Appendices.

When running the group

6 Record attendance at sessions, see page 7.
7 When the first session starts tell the children how special their group is.

This is an opportunity to give lots of positive messages.

8 Follow the golden keys: Pause, Ponder, Use Praise Phrases, slow the Pace.
9 At the end of each half-term reassess the children on the scales you have chosen and review the group and individual targets.
10 For the last group session include a farewell followed up with drawings of things the children have especially enjoyed so that they have a concrete reminder for as long as they need it.

Using the materials: flexibility

When using the materials go by the level that you feel your group of children have reached. There will be some groups of children who need repetition of sessions and some groups who need to start sessions at a higher level.

All groups of children can vary in their needs and you may find that in one nursery the children work happily at the earlier sessions whereas in another they have mastered the basic concepts therein and need to work on the concepts contained in the later sessions.

In our experience some sessions will sometimes need to be repeated three or more times, whereas another session at the same level is assimilated at the first presentation.

Further reading

Barnes, D. and Todd, G. (1977) *Language and Communication in Small Groups.* London: Routledge & Kegan Paul.

Cheshire County Council Website. http://www.salt.cheshire.gov.uk

Gardner, H. (1993a) *Frames of Mind: The Theory of Multiple Intelligences.* Canada: HarperCollins Canada.

Gardner, H. (1993b) *Multiple Intelligences: The Theory in Practice.* Canada: HarperCollins Canada.

Goodlad, J. (1984) *A Place Called School: Prospects for the Future.* NY: McGraw-Hill.

Kann Yeok-Hwa, N. (1998) *Enhancing Student Thinking Through Collaborative Learning.* Eric Digests ED422586 (Internet).

Kemple, K. M. (1992) *Understanding and Facilitating Pre-school Children's Peer Acceptance.* Eric Digests ED345866 (Internet).

Mosley, J. (1993) *Turn Your School Round.* Cambridge: LDA.

Mosley, J. (1996) *Quality Circle Time in the Primary School.* Cambridge: LDA.

Sizer, T. (1984) *Horace's Compromise.* Boston: Houghton Mifflin.

Stevens, P. W. Richards (2002) Eric Digests ED345929 (Internet).

Resources

Talkabout series; Talkabout the Playground; Pragmatics; Feelings

The Mr Badger Map is available from Black Sheep Press, 67 Middleton, Cowling, Keighley, West Yorks BD22 0DQ
Tel: 01535 631346
Email: alan@blacksheeppress.co.uk
www.blacksheep-epress.com

King and Hedgehog puppets (and many more) available from:
The Puppet Company Ltd, Unit 2, Cam Centre, Wilbury Way, Hitchin, Hertfordshire SG4 0TW
Tel: 01462 446040
www.puppetsbypost.com

Spirals language development group attendance record

Date of session	Session no.	Run by	Children who attended

Name .... **Class** ....

Please could you write a brief description about the child's present level of attainment in each of the following skills. You will be asked to repeat this activity in six weeks, therefore it would be helpful if, during the time, you could note any significant developments in any of the following areas and write them down.
Thank you.

Skill	Present level (1)	Present level (2)
Thinking skills Awareness and use of problem-solving strategies		
Language skills Use and understanding of language related to maths		
Social skills Attitude and response towards peers		
Listening skills Ability to listen and concentrate in class/group situations		
Classroom Confidence, responses and general performance in the classroom		

Materials that need preparation prior to sessions

Session 1

- Large soft ball.
- Counting cards with **dots** (not numbers) shown on both sides of the cards. Dots from one to seven or eight depending on the number of people in the group. There needs to be one card per person.
- Spotty dog mask.
- Thirty-second egg timer.
- Feely bag or other container with three objects in it.

Session 2

- Large soft ball.
- Large dice with pictures of one, two or three bears on each face.
- Separate cards of one, two or three bears to match above.
- Large cut-out cardboard fish.
- Five cards with spots one to five.
- Interesting box containing a cut-out number two (the number should have two dots on it for reference).

Session 3

- Large dice with teddy bears on the faces of the dice. **Use only one, two and three bears.**
- Large soft ball.
- Zebra and bear or two other animals.
- One shape for each person in the group (circle, triangle, square the same colour). For a later game you will need one triangle or circle for each person in the group.
- Thirty-second sand egg timer, and one building block for each person in the group.
- High-sided box containing four interesting objects.

Session 4

- Large soft ball.
- Spotty dog pictures.
- Collection of plastic plates and cups.
- Thirty-second sand egg timer.
- High sided box containing three interesting objects.

Session 5

- Soft toy hedgehog (another animal could be used if you can't find a hedgehog).
- King puppet or bossy character puppet.
- One shape for each person in the group (circle, triangle or square).
- Thirty-second sand egg timer, and building blocks in a box. One block for each person in the group.
- High-sided box containing three interesting objects.

Session 6

- Circles, square and triangle shapes (one for each person in the group) in a feely bag.
- Large A3 paper circle, paper triangle and two paper squares.
- Hedgehog and King puppets, one square shape, one paper square shape and felt-tip pen.
- Thirty-second sand egg timer and a box of bricks to build a tower.
- Spotted dice and counters which can be placed on the dice to cover the spots (or on the floor beside it).

Session 7

- Interesting box which contains the numerals two and three (the numbers should have two or three dots on them for reference).
- Hedgehog and King puppets.
- Two shapes (triangle and square made of carpet tiles work well).
- Number cards one to eight.
- Cut-out fish.

Session 8

- Assorted objects (one for each person) in a feely bag. (We want the children to identify what shapes they can see in these objects (e.g. can, ball, box, Sellotape, jewellery, patterned materials) and include some soft textures (e.g. cushions, furry materials).
- Five to ten plastic bottles on a box (appropriate number for group).
- Box of building bricks, two 30-second sand egg timers.
- Sealed packet of sequins or buttons.
- Plate of stones/plate of feathers – can be got from a coloured feather duster.

If you cannot get hold of these use rubber bands!

- Toy zebra and bear (or other toys as available).

Session 9

- Jar containing 25 small objects (e.g. plastic bricks, small animals, buttons).
- Numbers two and three, enough for everyone to have one numeral each.
- Feely bag.
- King and hedgehog puppets.
- Large square and triangle (carpet squares work well).
- Collection of plastic plates and cups.
- Two ribbons of the same length.
- Identical small objects to cover the ribbons lengthways.

Session 10

- Large square of material (e.g. table cloth).
- A little plastic bottle or pot for each child in the group plus one extra (small yoghurt pots are ideal for this).
- Spotty dog mask and dotted cards with numerals on one side (one card for each person in the group).
- Toy animal.
- One set of coloured cards in pairs: two red, two blue, two green, and so on (one card for each person).
- Two plates (plastic or paper).
- Pile of stones.
- Pile of feathers.

Session 11

- Feely bag with two ribbons – one long and one short – and a toy animal.
- Ice-cream cut-outs individually from the resources page (you could use large counters and call them biscuits!).
- A jar of small plastic animals, approximately three to four for each person in the group.
- Number cards zero to eight in numerals (one for each person in the group).
- Toy animal.
- Tambourine.

Session 12

- Feely bag containing three ribbons of different lengths.
- One toy animal.
- Set of numbered cards with dots beside the numbers. Two of each number for matching game.
- Large circle of material.
- Cut-out fish.

Session 13

- Interesting box containing a number three cut-out.
- Feely bag.
- Large number three cut out of a large piece of cloth or paper.
- Three plates – one with a building brick (plastic or wood) on, one with a pile of stones on and one with feathers on.
- Large square cloth.
- King and hedgehog puppets.

Session 14

- Large soft ball.
- Large rectangular cloth (table cloth or remnant).
- Six toy animals of different heights.
- Divided dots/numerals on cards – one per person in the group.

Session 15

- Large square cloth.
- Interesting box containing a triangle shape and a square shape.
- Three triangles.
- Three ribbons of different lengths.
- Spotty dog pictures.
- Dotted/numbered cards.
- Red and blue circles, enough for each child to have one each.

Session 16

- One large object and one small object to pass around.
- Number cards – one for each person in the group.
- King and hedgehog puppets.
- Big round cloth or circle of paper.
- Number box with numerals three and four.
- A circle for each person in the group.

Session 17

- Dotted/numeral cards.
- Same-sized square for each person in the group.
- Cube with a stick-on face on each face of the cube.
- Five toy animals.
- Cards zero, one, two, three.
- Tambourine.

Session 18

- Square shape in a box.

- Spotty dog pictures and spot number cards.
- Dotted counting cards.
- Cube shape.
- Hedgehog puppet.
- Thick pen.

Session 19

- Circle shape in a box.
- Same-sized square for each person.
- A cube.
- Two animals.
- Balance scales.
- Dotted numeral cards.
- A shape for each person in the group – circle or triangle (all the same colour).

Session 20

- Balance scales.
- Jar with small objects in.
- Dice.
- King and hedgehog puppets.
- Felt-tip pen and A3 square of paper.
- Cube-shaped cardboard box.
- Three fluffy animals.
- Various cardboard shapes (circle, semicircle, square, triangle, rectangle and star).

Session 21

- Wooden or plastic circles (enough for one per person in the group).
- Cylinder shape (may be unopened tin or packet).
- Cardboard tubes (kitchen paper or toilet roll tubes).
- Clean paper and pencil.
- Three cube-shaped objects for each person in the group plus one more.
- A set of matching number cards, zero zero, one one, two two and so on.
- Toy bear.

Session 22

- Number cards.
- Ten objects to arrange into piles.
- Weasel and bear.
- Four toy animals.
- Jar containing objects.
- Two triangles – one regular with equal sides, one irregular with one side longer.

Session 23

- Number cards.
- Three cloth shapes to hide wooden shapes underneath.
- Red and blue wooden or plastic shapes, one for each person in the group (e.g. rectangle, star, circle, triangle and square).
- King and hedgehog puppets.
- Two yellow hoops.
- Jar of objects.
- Toy animals.

Session 24

- Large cloth.
- Addy the Adder (a little snake puppet with a plus sign on her back can be made with a sock pulled over your hand).
- Hedgehog and King puppets.
- Solid cube shape and flat square shape.
- Number cards, one for each person in the group.

Session 25

- Three cubes for each person in the group plus one extra.
- Toy bear.
- Yellow hoops.
- Large cloth.
- Red and blue square and triangle shapes to share around the group.
- Three toy animals.
- Objects in a jar.
- Addy the Adder (a little snake puppet with a plus sign on her back).
- Sid the Subtractor (a little snake puppet with a minus sign on his back).

Session 26

- Addy the Adder (a little snake puppet with a plus sign on her back).
- Sid the Subtractor (a little snake puppet with a minus sign on his back).
- Large cloth.

Session 27

- Number card for each person in the group.
- Two toys (one has a badge with one object on, the other has a badge with two objects on to represent odd and even). You could make them different colours if you wish.
- Hedgehog and King puppets.
- Three cloth shapes – triangular, square and circular.
- Assorted wooden or plastic shapes.
- Circles – one for each person (red and blue).

Session 28

- Interesting box containing numbers two and five.
- Robot mask.
- Large piece of paper and pen.
- Spotted dice and small objects which may be put on the dice to cover the spots.

Session 29

- Three cloths – triangular, circular and square.
- Wooden or plastic shapes – triangular, circular and square.
- Large cloth.
- Addy the Adder and Sid the Subtractor puppets.
- Number cards.

Session 30

- Robot mask.
- Square piece of material.
- Tambourine.
- Felt-tip pen and A3 sheet of paper.

Session 31

- Squares and triangles in a basket.
- Zebra and bear or two other animals.
- Cards one to ten (one per person in the group).
- Two toys with a one- or two-star badge.

Session 32

- Mr Bear soft toy.
- Five piles of small objects.
- Weasel puppet (or other).
- One extra soft toy animal.
- Balance scales.

Session 33

- Large piece of paper.
- Dotted counting cards.
- Spotty dog mark.
- Weasel puppet.
- Lion cub puppet.
- Two badges with either one star or two stars.
- Three squares of cardboard.

Session 34

- Tambourine.
- Robot mask.
- Large square of material.
- Masks.
- Addy the Adder and Sid the Subtractor (two little sock puppets plus and minus).
- Lion cub puppet.
- Five squares of cardboard, three should be dark.
- Three toy frogs.

Session 35

- Map.
- Badger puppet.
- Toy bear.
- Four frog puppets or toys.
- Shape objects in a feely bag.
- Five plus one cubes for each child in the group.
- Four plastic or toy frogs for each child in the group.

Session 36

- Map.
- Badger puppet.
- Jar containing small animals (plastic or paper).

Session Notes

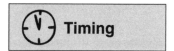

are listed in the introduction. Most are readily available in nurseries and classrooms; others are provided as appendices.

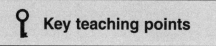

Twenty to thirty minutes depending on the length of time spent on each game.

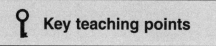

It is essential to keep the pace of your language slow. Use 'pondering' to gain attention and interest and to slow down the pace. Also essential is keeping language as uncluttered and simple as possible.

Visual cues

Children have different learning strengths. Some learn best from hearing information, some from having it presented visually and some from activity-based tasks. Pre-school children especially learn best when all three aspects are present and learning is substantially supported by visual materials and activities and rhythm. For this reason the sessions are designed to be active and visual with familiar rhymes. You can help the process greatly by using simple gestures to accompany descriptions and instructions.

Praise

Praise every child at least twice in each session.

Praise for good sitting before the group becomes too fidgety. Offer to sprinkle imaginary 'magic glue dust' for a child who has difficulty in sitting still.

Positive

Try not to say, 'No, that's wrong.' Clearly there are right and wrong answers, but the group works on similar principles to brainstorming where all ideas are listened to and considered, and then an answer is chosen from all the ideas. We tend to say, 'Thank you, you spoke up really well. You gave me another idea.'

Giving time to think

When you expect a child to answer a question give him or her at least 15 seconds to respond. (You will be surprised how long that seems!) Encourage with comments such as:

You are thinking really well. Well done!

You are quiet and you are thinking about this really well!

If the child doesn't answer, offer support by asking:

Would you like some help from us?

If yes, ask the group (adults included) to put up their hands if they want to help give an answer. The child then chooses someone.

Fun

Enjoy this time with the children.

Behaviour

Try, when changing the activity and the pace of the activity, to change the focus and distract from negative behaviour if it occurs. Praise the other children for behaviour that you do want to see. Try not to introduce a competitive element.

Mathematical language introduced in this book

Vocabulary introduced, then developed through the Spirals programme

Session 1	one, two, three, four, five, count to, one, spot, beginning, end, first, last, whole, more, one more, circle, triangle, square, side, corner, corners, swap, time, how many, good guess
Session 2	same, match, top, count, roll, how many
Session 3	how many times, one more time, next, I have five things, nearly, next and pattern, equal, unequal, fair
Session 4	different, fast, faster, slow, slowly, guess, estimate
Session 5	shape, curved side, change, yellow circle, red triangle, long curved side, high
Session 6	bigger, shapes with three sides, shapes with a blue face, shapes with a green face, few, lots
Session 7	face, top, start at the top, choose, turn
Session 8	all together, count together, heavy, light, more than, equal, unequal, same as me
Session 9	three corners, three sides, same length
Session 10	across, diagonal, line, it's not the same, on, along, another, sets
Session 11	long, short, first in line, last in line
Session 12	one straight side, semicircle, half a circle
Session 13	heaviest, lightest, rectangle, long sides, short sides, longer
Session 14	four sides, four corners, biggest, largest, tallest, smallest, adding, more, half
Session 15	longest, shortest
Session 16	round, more than
Session 17	zero, cube, take turns
Session 18	who has got, about the same, less than, before and after

Vocabulary developed through Spirals programme

Session 19   heaviest, lightest, behind, weigh, weighing

Session 20   one too many, two too many, one less, one left over, too few

Session 21   enough, each

Session 22   missing, line up in order, zero, check

Session 23   even numbers, odd numbers, give me clues

Session 24   morning, add, solid shape, flat shape, odd, even

Session 25   groups, if

Session 26   later, take some away, added

Session 27   lunch-time

Session 28   forward, backward, sideways, middle, afternoon

Session 29   evening

Session 30   night-time

Session 31   when, towards the middle, forward, backward, sideways

Session 32   missing, heavier weight

Session 33   today, yesterday

Session 34   right, left

Session 35   daytime, night-time, along, beside, round the corner, almost there, a little way further, first, second, third, fourth, row

Session 36   line, row

Session 1

Materials

- Large soft ball.
- Counting cards with **dots** (not numbers) shown on both sides of the cards. Dots from one to seven or eight depending on the number of people in the group. There needs to be one card per person.
- Spotty dog mask and two dog pictures.
- Thirty-second egg-timer.
- Feely bag or other container with three objects in it.

Roll the ball

(Sitting)

Sit together in a circle. Praise children for sitting well and looking at you ready to listen.

Say you want to find out everyone's name. You will be rolling the ball to each other and saying your name and the name of the person you will be rolling the ball to. For example, *'My name is Angela and I am rolling the ball to Tom.'* Continue until everyone has had at least one turn.

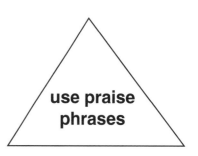

use praise phrases

Counting

(Sitting)

Introduce the spotty dog and say that you will be playing a game with him and that he will need to know you can count. Encourage one of the children to count the people in the group, include themselves in the counting, and say the numbers out loud. (Encourage children to take a turn to do this in order to check their ability to count out loud with one-to-one correspondence. Adults also count themselves in to provide a good model.)

Spotty dog

(Standing)

One of the adults holds the spotty dog picture and dog without spots. The dog has to collect his spots. He needs to collect one spot first then his spots from the head down towards the tail. Ask, *'Who has got one spot? Come and wear the spotty dog mask. Who has got two spots? ... come and stand behind ...'* and so on, making a line to represent the spotty dog. Encourage the children to identify this by themselves. Children with more spots are at the 'tail end' – as in the picture.

When *everyone* is in the line:

Ask which person is **first** and which person **last** – who has a few spots – as the front/head of the dog, who has more spots – as the tail end of the dog.

Then act out a little story together of the dog sniffing through the grass wagging his tail (hands behind their backs). He yawns and stretches, and curls up to have a sleep.

Shape game

(Sitting, then standing)

Using the large shapes from the feely bag hand the first one to a person in the circle. Hand out the other shapes, one to each person in the pattern – **circle, triangle, square,** and so on. Each time ask if the children know the name of the shape.

Stand up and play the Swap Game.

Say,

'Triangles, hands up; circles, hands on ears; squares turn around' and so on until the children are confident with the name of their shape.

- Then encourage children to swap or change places:
  'Triangles swap places'
  'Circles swap places'

Now stimulate use of the vocabulary by encouraging children to choose the category (e.g. 'circles swap places').

If the child can only say 'circles' accept this and note that practice is needed in extending language in future session.

Play time

(Sitting)

Use the 30-second egg timer. Say, *'This is an egg timer. It tells us how much time has passed. This is a half-minute or thirty second timer.'* Watch the action of the sand as a group.

Then say that you are going to see how many times the group can sing *Heads and shoulders knees and toes*...before the sand all runs down to the bottom of the timer. This will take about half a minute. Turn over the egg timer.

Sing the song with actions.

> Heads and shoulders knees and toes, knees and toes.
> Heads and shoulders knees and toes, knees and toes.
> Eyes and ears, and mouth and nose.
> Heads and shoulders knees and toes,
> Knees and toes.

Talk about how much of the song you were able to sing in half a minute/thirty seconds before the sand ran through.

Pass the guessing box

(Standing)

Pass around a high-sided box with three items in it. Ask the children to look in the box and count how many items are in it. Tell the children to use their eyes not their fingers. Ask each person *'How many things can you see in the box? Have a good guess.'* Praise good guesses but make no further comment.

Closing round – Pass a smile

(Standing)

Put on a sad face, then send a happy smile around the circle.

relax and
have fun

BE
POSITIVE

Session 2

Materials

- Large soft ball.
- Large dice with pictures of one, two or three bears on each face.
- Separate cards of one, two or three bears to match above.
- Large cut-out cardboard fish.
- Five cards with spots one to five.
- Interesting box containing a cut-out number two (the number should have two dots on it for reference).

Roll the ball

(Sitting)

Say you want to find out everyone's name. You will be rolling the ball to each other and saying your name and the name of the person you will be rolling the ball to. For example, *'My name is Angela and I am rolling the ball to Phillip.'* Continue until everyone has had at least one turn.

Roll the teddy bear dice

(Sitting)

Roll the dice into the middle of the circle saying, *'Let's watch where the dice lands. Look at the top of the dice – it shows three bears. Let's count them – one, two, three. Now you can roll the dice.'*

Offer a turn to each child around the circle. Encourage the children to roll the dice and look at the top face of the dice and count the bears. Next, model rolling the dice to a child in the group saying their name and asking how many teddy bears they can see, for example, *'Tom – How many teddies?'*

Tom counts the bears and tells the group how many he can see. Give each person in the group the chance to roll the dice and tell you how many bears they can see.

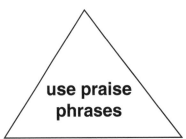

use praise phrases

Matching the bears

(Sitting)

When everyone (including the adults) has had a turn at rolling the dice bring out the matching pictures of one, two and three bears. The tasks now are to roll the dice, count the bears and then point to the matching pictures.

Emphasise the words **same** and **match**. For example, say, *'This picture matches the one on the dice. The two pictures are the same: they match don't they?'*

Encourage the children to ask other children, *'Does my picture match? Is it the same?'*

Number song

(Standing)

Hold up the cut-out fish and tell the group, *'You are going to sing a song about catching a fish – one, two, three, four, five, once I caught a fish alive.'*

Hold up the fish and say, *'And I give the fish to Claire.'*

Then we all sing – *'one, two, three, four, five, once I caught a fish alive.'* And Claire holds up the fish and says, *'And I give the fish to Andrew.'*

And so on until everyone has had a turn.

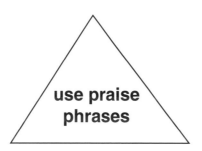

Spots before your eyes

(Sitting)

Lay out the spotted cards one to five in a line across the middle of the circle. Count the spots on them together.

Then choose individual children to find the cards you name. They pick up the card, count the spots, then put the card back and sit down again.

'Find a card with three spots on it'.
'Find a card with four spots on it' and so on.

Praise for effort. If a child chooses the wrong card, do not comment but repeat the request with another child on the next but one turn. At the end of the game stand by each card and count the spots out loud yourself.

Growing numbers

(Active)

All crouch on the floor.

Count 'one, two, three, four, and five', as you all get taller. Then stretch your arms right up when you get to five. Jump once and all clap hands.

Number box

(Sitting)

Bring out the interesting box. Say, *'I've got a number in my box – can you guess what it is?'* Allow the children to guess. Then say, *'I'll give you a clue.'*

Show them the card with two spots and say, *'This tells us what the number is. It's number…two!'*

Model running your finger around it saying: *'two.'* Count the dots on it. Pass it around the circle for each child to do the same. Emphasise the top of the number as the starting point.

Closing round – Pass a smile

(Standing)

Put on a sad face, then send a happy smile around the circle.

BE
POSITIVE

use
pondering
take your
time

Session 3

Materials

- Large dice with teddy bears on the faces of the dice. **Use only one, two and three bears.**
- Large soft ball.
- Zebra and bear or two other animals.
- One shape for each person in the group (circle, triangle, square the same colour). For a later game you will need one triangle or circle for each person in the group.
- Thirty-second sand egg timer, and one building block for each person in the group.
- High-sided box containing four interesting objects.

Roll the ball

(Sitting)

Say you want to find out everyone's name. You will be rolling the ball to each other and saying your name and the name of the person you will be rolling the ball to (e.g. *'My name* is *Celestine and I am rolling the ball to Tom').* Continue until everyone has had at least one turn.

Roll the teddy bear dice

(Sitting)

Roll the dice into the middle of the circle saying, *'Let's watch where the dice lands. Look at the top of the dice – it shows three bears. Lets count them – one, two, three. Now you can roll the dice.'*

Offer turns around the circle. Encourage the children to roll the dice and look at the top face of the dice and count the bears. Say your name and roll the dice to a child in the group, saying their name and asking how many teddy bears they can see on the top face of the dice; for example, *'Sean – How many teddies?'*

Sean counts the bears and tells the group how many he can see. Give each person in the group the chance to roll the dice and tell you how many bears they can see. They then roll it to the next person asking, *'How many bears?'*

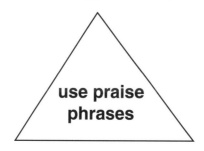

use praise phrases

27

Shape basket

(Standing)

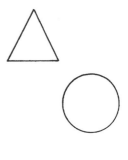

Give out triangles and circles and squares (one for each person). Talk about sides and corners. Use the 'slide down the side' and 'touch a corner' as memory joggers.

Then play the game, saying, *'Triangles, hands up, circles, hands on ears, squares turn around'* and so on until children are confident with the names of the shapes.

Next encourage children to swap or change places.

- Triangles change places.
- Circles change places.

Now stimulate use of the vocabulary by encouraging children to give the instructions; for example, 'Circles change places.' Gradually encourage a lengthening of this phrase ('Circles change places when I clap my hands').

Understanding time

(Sitting)

Remind the group about the sand egg timer game in the last session and how the timer told us how much time we had to sing a song:

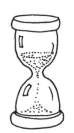

- *'We had to sing the song before the sand ran down. How many times did we sing the song?'*
- *'Last time we saw how many times you could sing a song and this time we are going to see how high we can build a tower before the sand runs through the timer.'*

Watch the action of a 30-second egg timer. Tell the group that now you are all going to see how high you can build a tower of bricks before the sand runs out.

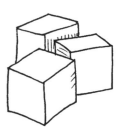

Pass a box of bricks around the group. Each person chooses a brick. Decide who will go first, then second, and so on. Tell the group to be as quiet as possible. Set the timer, then start taking turns to build the tower.

At the end talk about the high tower we have all built. Choose a child to count the bricks then put the bricks back into the box.

Zebra and bear share

(Sitting)

Bring in two animals to 'help' put the bricks away. Give them each unequal amounts, then role-play the zebra, for example, saying, *'You have more than me, that's not fair. We should have the same!'*

The other animal agrees and then gives the zebra most of their bricks. Then after a pause the other animal says, *'Wait; now you have more than me, that's not fair! That's not equal, that's unequal!'*

Ask for ideas on how to make it fair. (One for you, one for me.) At the end of the game pass the animals around for the children to stroke.

use pondering take your time

Rhyme time

(Walking around and singing)

All walk around in a circle and sing:

> One, two, three, four, five, once I caught a fish alive, six, seven, eight, nine, ten, then I let it go again.

Stop and say:

> Because it bit my finger.

Say, 'Let's sing this one more time.' Repeat, then sit down.
All sit down.

Nearly there

(Standing)

Place a green shape at your feet. Tell a simple story about two animals who try to jump on to the shape. Choose two children to play the animal parts. Place a red shape on the floor as a starting point. Give a toy animal to two children to hold. Ask the two children to take turns, in taking one jump at a time each one holding an animal as they do so. Use the phrases 'nearly there' and 'getting nearer' as they approach the green shape: 'The rabbit is nearly there.'

Afterwards see if anyone can remember how many jumps each animal made. Ponder with the children about why the jumps may have been different.

Closing round – Patterns

(Sitting in a semicircle to leave a space for children to line up)

Place circles of two different colours in a group on the floor in front of you. Ask one child to choose a circle and stand up in the space in front.

Then ask another child to take a circle of a different colour and to stand next to the first child. Repeat this to establish a pattern of alternative colours. Talk about the pattern they are making. Ask what colour is next. Talk again about the pattern. Ask each child what colour will be next. Ask the next child to choose that colour and to stand in the line in the right place. Encourage the children to complete a pattern. Alternatively, ask each child to pick up two circles of different colours and to hold one in each hand – or place circles in front of them on the floor. This will establish a pattern more quickly.

Then say, 'You are all in a line, let's get into a circle.' Go back into a semicircle and do a round with each child saying the name of their colour out loud.

Session 4

Materials
- Large soft ball.
- Spotty dog pictures.
- Collection of plastic plates and cups.
- Thirty-second sand egg timer.
- High sided box containing three interesting objects.

Roll the ball

(Sitting)

Roll the ball across the circle saying *'My name is Robert and I'm rolling the ball to Sally'* until everyone has had a turn.

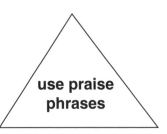

use praise
phrases

Spotty dog

(Standing)

One of the adults holds the spotty dog picture and dog without spots. The dog has to collect his spots. He needs to collect one spot first then his spots from the head down towards the tail. Ask, *'Who has got one spot? Come and hold the picture of the spotty dog. Who has got two spots?... come and stand behind...'* and so on, making a line to represent the spotty dog. Encourage the children to identify this by themselves. Children with more spots are at the 'tail end' – as in the picture.

When *everyone* is in the line:

Ask which person is **first** and which person **last** – who has a few spots – as the front/head of the dog, who has more spots – as the tail end of the dog.

Then act out a little story together of the dog sniffing through the grass wagging his tail (hands behind their backs). He yawns and stretches, and curls up to have a sleep.

Same/different

(Sitting)

Have a collection of objects in a box (plates and cups, plastic spoons). Children have to take three things from the box, two the same and one different. Encourage the children to say which of their choices are the same and which are different. Talk about how the items differ by appearance and use. For example, two cups are the same because you drink from them, but the saucer is different because you put the cup on it. However, one cup and saucer may be the same because they are blue and the other cup different because it is red. Put the items back and the next person has a turn.

Nearly there

(Standing)

Place a green shape at your feet. Tell a simple story about two animals who try to jump on to the shape. Choose two children to play the part of the animals. Place a red shape on the floor as a starting point. Give a toy animal to two children to hold. Ask the two children to take turns making one jump at a time. Use the word 'nearly' as in nearly there: *'The rabbit is nearly there.'*

Afterwards see if anyone can remember how many jumps each animal made. Ponder with the children about why they may have made a different number of jumps. Encourage use of long, longest, short, shortest, big, biggest.

Playtime

(Sitting)

Show the children a sand egg timer. Talk about it telling us how much time it takes to do things. Talk about the last time you played this game. Ponder on whether you would sing more of the song if you sing quickly.

Say, *'We are going to see how long it takes us to sing a song this time.'* Turn the timer upside down and all watch the sand as it goes through.

Sing the action song:

> Heads and shoulders, knees and toes, knees and toes,
> Heads and shoulders knees and toes, knees and toes,
> Eyes and ears and mouth and nose,
> Heads and shoulders knees and toes,
> Knees and toes.

Continue until the sand runs out. Talk about the time it has taken us and how many times we sang the song. Do one more, varying the speed at which you sing: **faster** or **slower**, and ponder on the effects.

Closing round – good guesses

Say that you are going to give a *'rough guess or estimate of how many items there are in the box'*. Pass around a high-sided guessing box containing three objects and ask how many things the children can see. Emphasise the need to use their eyes only and not touch. No comment is made on the children's estimates except what good guesses there have been.

Praise children's guesses.

> **use
> pondering
> take your
> time**

Session 5

Materials

- Soft toy hedgehog (another animal could be used if you can't find a hedgehog).
- King puppet or bossy character puppet.
- One shape for each person in the group (circle, triangle or square).
- Thirty-second sand egg timer, and building blocks in a box. One block for each person in the group.
- High-sided box containing three interesting objects.

Helping the Maths Hedgehog

(Sitting)

Say hello to the Maths Hedgehog. Make him appear shy. Say that he wants to know the name of the children. Go around the circle asking the group to tell him their names. (If any child tries to touch the hedgehog while you hold him, explain that he is shy and might get frightened. This is in order to establish a calm, enabling atmosphere.)

Then say, *'There's a young Hedgehog here who is learning all about shapes. Perhaps we can help?'*

Give the hedgehog a square shape. Run your finger along the side and say that he wants to know what this part of the square is called. Ask if anyone can remember.

Whether children say side or shape or something else, just accept this and ponder on what they have said, e.g. *'Mmm, you think it may be a shape?' (Or 'side?')* When all who want to give an answer have done so say that, *'yes, it is a side'*.

Introduce the King puppet and say that he asks the Maths hedgehog questions about shape. Talk about the King being a bit bossy sometimes and the hedgehog being shy. Say that we can help the hedgehog to find good answers.

The King asks the hedgehog what the straight parts of the square are called. The hedgehog answers correctly and looks pleased.

Next the King asks: *'**How many sides** does the square shape have?'* The hedgehog runs his paw around the sides and counts one, two, three, four, five, six, by going round too many times. *'Stop'*, says the King, *'You have gone around the shape too many times Hedgehog! Let me help. Hold it here in the corner [demonstrate]. Slide your finger along each side. Remember – "slide along the side".'*

Model the correct way by placing the shape on the floor and putting one finger on a corner and counting the sides. Emphasise the need to stop when you get to the point where your finger is. Talk about how hard this can be.

> **use pondering take your time**

Pass the square shape to each person in the group. Ask them to 'slide along a side' using a finger. Then ask how many sides there are and note whether they can count the sides accurately. No comment is made at this stage beyond an interested 'Mmm...'.

The hedgehog then counts the sides correctly and is praised by the King. The King goes away.

Pass the Hedgehog around for a hug from each person in the group. Then carefully sit him on a shelf away from the group.

(Always treat the puppets with respect for their characters or they will lose their character in the children's eyes and may not be as effective in engaging children in the group activities.)

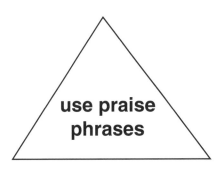

Shape basket

(Standing)

Hand out triangles and circle and square shapes – one for each person.

Talk about sides and corners as before. Use the memory joggers 'Slide around the side' and 'Touch a corner'. (The circle doesn't have sides or corners.)

Play the shape game

(Standing)

Say, *'Triangles, hands up, circles, hands on ears, squares turn around'* and so on until the group are confident with their shape.

Then encourage shapes to swap or change places:

- Triangles change places.
- Circles change places.

Then change instructions to:

- Shapes with four sides change places.
- Shapes with three sides change places.
- Shapes with no sides or corners change places.

Now stimulate use of the vocabulary by encouraging children to give the instructions; for example, *'Circles change places.'*

All sit down.

Ask the children one by one to put their shape on a pile in the middle of the circle by saying, *'You will need to listen carefully now. I want a yellow circle.'* Place it on the floor in front of you. *'I want a red triangle.'* Add it to the pile. *'I want a shape with no sides or corners',* and so on.

Say, *'You did that so well. We will make a tower now with bigger shapes.'*

Play time – Marking the passing of time

(Sitting)

Ask the group what they remember about this game.

Watch the action of a 30-second sand egg timer. Tell the group you are all going to see how high you can build a tower of bricks again before the sand runs out of the top of the timer. The sand timer will tell us how long it takes us.

Pass around a box of bricks. Each person chooses a brick and passes the box on to the next person. Decide who will go first and which way around you are going. Tell the group to be as quiet as possible. Set the timer, then start taking turns to build the tower.

At the end talk about the high tower we have all built. Ask a child to count how many people there are in the group and how many bricks there should be in the tower. Give time to ponder, then count the bricks together and say, for example: *'Yes there are eight people and eight bricks'* (that is, one each).

Choose someone sitting well to put the bricks back into the box.

Number train

(Standing)

All walk around in a big circle counting and ending with steam train noise.

> One, two, three, four, five Whoo Whoo,
> One, two, three, four, five, Whoo Whoo ....

**relax and
have fun**

Closing round – Pass the guessing box

(Sitting)

Say, *'We are going to guess or estimate how many things are in the box.'*

Pass around a high-sided box which contains six interesting objects, and ask children for ideas as to how many they think there are. Emphasise the need to use their eyes only and not touch. No comment is made on the children's estimates except what good guesses there have been.

Session 6

Materials

- Circles, square and triangle shapes (one for each person in the group) in a feely bag.
- Large A3 paper circle, paper triangle and two paper squares.
- Hedgehog and King puppets, one square shape, one paper square shape and felt-tip pen.
- Thirty-second sand egg timer and a box of bricks to build a tower.
- Spotted dice and counters which can be placed on the dice to cover the spots (or on the floor beside it).

Pass shapes in a feely bag

(Sitting)

Ask children to take out one shape from the feely bag. Encourage them to name the shape and then to show you how many sides the shape has. Encourage use of 'slide along the side'. Then the children should count the sides and next ask how many corners they think there are. Use the 'Touch a corner' memory jogger.

Helping the Maths Hedgehog

(Sitting)

Explain that the King is going to ask the Maths Hedgehog about the square shape again. The hedgehog says he thinks he knows the answer but asks if he could be passed round and have the children whisper quietly what they think the straight parts of the square shape are called. When the King comes in and asks the question, the hedgehog says he knows the word starts with an **s** sound, and it is **spiders!** As a group enjoy helping the hedgehog to remember the right answer of **sides**.

The King then asks if the hedgehog knows what the pointed bits where the sides join are called. Pass the square shape around for the children to feel. Take ideas. The hedgehog then answers 'Corners!' and is praised by the King.

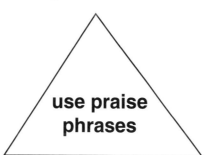

use praise
phrases

Patterns

(Sitting in a semicircle to leave a space for children to line up)

Lay out the pattern the group made last time and leave it there on one side for comparison. *'We are going to make a different pattern.'* Now lay out a set of circles and triangles in a group on the floor. Ask one child to choose a shape and to stand up in the space in the circle.

Then ask another child to take a shape and stand next to the first child. Talk about the pattern they are making, for example, it may be circle, circle or triangle, triangle or circle, triangle. Ask what shape is next. Talk again about the pattern. Ask each child what shape will be next. Ask the next child to choose that shape and stand in the line in the right place. Encourage the children to complete a pattern. Go back into a semi-circle and do a round with each child saying the name of their shape out loud.

**use
pondering
take your
time**

Standing on shapes

(Standing)

Lay out the large paper shapes – circle, triangle and square. Choose a shape to stand on and name each one.

Ask the children to stand in a line. Ask the first child to choose which shape they want to stand on. When they say the word *'Triangle'* or *'Circle'* or *'Square'*, encourage them to stand on the corresponding shape (if the child stands on a different shape from the one they've named just note it to yourself and move on – the child may need some extra practice in the classroom).

Give each person in the group several turns.

Roll the spotted dice with corresponding objects

(Sitting, using eyes not fingers)

Throw the dice – count the spots on the face of the dice by *looking* not touching. Choose counters to correspond with the number of spots. Then put these counters on the spots one by one (or at the side).

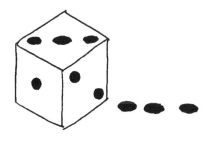

Choose one too many when it is your turn. Talk about *'One too many'*; *'Take away one'*; *'One less'*; *'Now they're the same – equal'*.

Finally, see if the children can recall how many spots each person had.

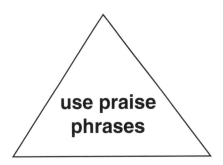

use praise phrases

Closing round – counting

(Standing)

Count round the group, then encourage each person to contribute one number out loud, so:

- First person says *'one'*.
- Second person says *'two'*.

Continue until everyone has had a turn.

BE POSITIVE

Session 7

> ## Materials
> - Interesting box which contains the numerals two and three (the numbers should have two or three dots on them for reference).
> - Hedgehog and King puppets.
> - Two shapes (triangle and square made of carpet tiles work well).
> - Number cards one to eight.
> - Cut-out fish.

Number box two and three

(Sitting)

Take the numbers out of an interesting box one at a time and pass them around the group. Encourage the children to run their fingers round the shapes and to say *'two'* then *'three'*. Adults model this as well, emphasising the need to start at the top of the number.

All about shapes

(Standing)

The hedgehog brings a square and a triangle to the group. Lay the shapes on the floor in the middle of the circle.

The hedgehog chooses children to say in turn which shape they want before they:

- Choose one shape and hold it.
- Show hedgehog a side using 'slide along the side' memory prompt.
- Tell hedgehog how many sides there are on their chosen shape.
- Show hedgehog a corner using 'the touch a corner' memory prompt. Tell the hedgehog how many corners there are on the shape.

The King comes in and says how hard the children and the hedgehog have worked. It is time for the hedgehog to have a nap.

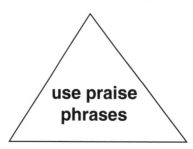

use praise
phrases

Number hops

(Standing)

Lay out the cards in a line one to eight (or the number of people in the group).

Choose individual children to stand on the first card. Tell them which card to hop or jump on to.

For example, *'Elli, stand on number one, now hop to number six.'* (The child must hop on to each of the cards on the way.) Comment on how many cards the children stood on and how many hops they did on the way.

Few and lots

(Sitting)

The King shows the hedgehog a jar of small items (counters, beads). He asks the hedgehog to give him a few. He turns his back and the hedgehog gives him several handfuls.

The King turns around as says, *'You've given me lots. I only want a few.'*

The hedgehog takes one away and asks, *'Is that a few?'*

The King says, *'No, that's still too many. I only want a few.'*

The hedgehog takes most of them away, leaving only a few for the King to comment on. Pass the jar around. The King asks each person for a few or lots.

Closing round – Number song

(Standing)

Hold up the cut-out fish and tell the group, *'You are going to sing a song about catching a fish.'*

Sing *'One, two, three, four, five, once I caught a fish alive.'*

Hold up the fish and say, *'And I give the fish to Claire.'*

Then we all sing *'One, two, three, four, five, once I caught a fish alive.'* Claire holds up the fish and says, *'And I give the fish to Andrew.'*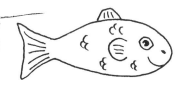

And so on until we have all had a turn.

BE
POSITIVE

Session 8

Materials

- Assorted objects (one for each person) in a feely bag. (We want the children to identify what shapes they can see in these objects (e.g. can, ball, box, Sellotape, jewellery, patterned materials) and include some soft textures (e.g. cushions, furry materials).
- Five to ten plastic bottles on a box (appropriate number for group).
- Box of building bricks, two 30-second sand egg timers.
- Sealed packet of sequins or buttons.
- Plate of stones/plate of feathers – can be got from a coloured feather duster. If you cannot get hold of these use rubber bands!
- Toy zebra and bear (or other toys as available).

Shape feely bag

(Sitting)

Pass around objects in a feely bag. Each person takes one object out and decides (with the group's help if necessary) what shapes they can see in it. Ask how you can tell it is a certain shape. Help children to talk about sides and corners (e.g. *'How can you know it's a square – yes, it has four sides and four corners'*). Slide along the sides and count them. Or *'Yes it's a circle. It has no corners'*.

At the end of this game gather in the shapes by asking, *'Can you give me a round blue shape with no corners, can you give me something with a square in it?'* Gather in the objects by describing the attributes of the objects. Simplify or extend these instructions in accordance with the needs of the group.

Rhyme and counting time

(Standing)

Place one bottle for each person on the wall (box). Walk around the box singing to the tune of 10 Green Bottles: *'10 little bottles standing on the wall and if one little bottle should accidentally fall'* (or *'5 little bottles...'* as appropriate to the needs of the group).

(Pause)

Choose a person to remove a bottle from the wall and ask the children to count how many bottles there are left. Continue singing and playing the game until all the bottles have gone.

**use
pondering
take your
time**

Counting

(Sitting)

Ask one child to stand up to count the people in the group (e.g. *'Lizzie, can you count how many people there are in the group?'* Then choose three people to stand up by saying, *'Sally, Chris and Kuli…stand up please.'* Ask Lizzie: *'How many people are standing up?'* (Ensure that the child includes herself.) If a child counts only children and not grown-ups bring this to their attention and work it out as a group that 'people' as a term includes both children and adults.

Then ask, *'How many people are sitting down?'*

Then ask, *'How many people **all together**'?* Indicate by using an inclusive hand and arm gesture.

Ask and ponder, *'If we all stand up, how many people will be standing up?'* Encourage answers, then all stand up and check, saying, *'Let's stand up and count together.'*

Coloured feathers and stones 'Heavy and Light'

(Sitting)

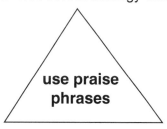

Pass a plate of stones around the circle. Talk about them being heavy.

Then pass a plate of feathers around the circle. Talk about them being light.

Talk about heavy and light. Pass both plates so that children can hold both at the same time. Ask them which one is heavier. Ask if it is harder to hold that plate up (one little boy in our group said about a plate of feathers *'Oh it is as light as a feather!'* This sort of analogy can be encouraged).

use praise phrases

Nearly there

(Standing)

Place a green shape at your feet. Tell a simple story about two animals who try to jump on to the shape. Choose two children to play the animal parts. Place a red shape on the floor as a starting point. Give a toy animal to the two children to hold. Ask the children to take turns, making one jump at a time. Use the word 'nearly' as in nearly there. *'The rabbit is nearly there.'*

Afterwards see if anyone can remember how many jumps each animal made. Ponder with the children about why the jumps may have been different.

Building time

(Sitting)

Talk about the last time you played this and what the sand egg timers tell you. Talk about how long it takes to do something.

Pass the box of bricks around the circle. Each person takes two bricks.

Reintroduce the idea of using the sand egg timer to see how many bricks the group can place on the tower. Explain that today you will have two bricks to place – ponder about whether you will need twice the time.

Give instructions as to how you want the game to be played, either by building a tower with each person in the circle putting their two bricks on to it, or taking turns to put one each in turn around the circle.

When playing this game turn the second timer over as soon as the first has run out.

Talk briefly about the results and **praise** for speed and co-operation.

Zebra and bear share

(Sitting)

Bring in two animals to 'help' put the bricks away. Give each animal unequal amounts, then role-play the zebra, for example, saying, *'You have more than me, that's not fair. We should have the same!'*

The other animal agrees and gives the zebra most of their bricks. Then after a pause the other animal says, *'Wait; now you have more than me, that's not fair! That's not equal, that's unequal!'*

Ask for ideas as to how to make it fair. At the end of the game pass the animals around for the children to stroke.

Closing round – Same as me game

(Standing)

All stand up in a circle and say, *'Watch me, I'm going to put my hands behind my back. Can you do the same as me?'*

Do a series of actions encouraging the children to perform the same actions (pat head, hop, turn around). Emphasise the word **same**.

Session 9

Materials

- Jar containing 25 small objects (e.g. plastic bricks, small animals, buttons).
- Numbers two and three, enough for everyone to have one numeral each.
- Feely bag.
- King and hedgehog puppets.
- Large square and triangle (carpet squares work well).
- Collection of plastic plates and cups.
- Two ribbons of the same length.
- Identical small objects to cover the ribbons lengthways.

Feely bag

(Sitting. Have beside you a container with 25 small objects in it)

Pass around the feely bag containing the numerals two and three. Each person takes out a numeral. Ask them to run their finger around it while saying what number it is. The children then take the corresponding number of objects from the jar and lay them on top of their numeral. Ponder on the relationship of the objects and the numeral (e.g. *'That is number two and there are two things on it and that is what two means.'*). Collect up the items at the end of the game.

Help the hedgehog

(Sitting)

Lay a square and a triangle on the floor. The hedgehog tells the children that he wants them to guess what shape he is thinking of. He will give clues to help them.

    For example, *'My shape has three corners and three sides'.* Occasionally the hedgehog forgets what he has said and asks the children to remind him by repeating it for him. Give each child a turn. Then the King comes in and praises the efforts of the hedgehog and the group. He asks before he goes if the shapes are the same or different.

Same/different

(Sitting)

Have a collection of plates and cups. Children have to take three things from the box, two the same and one different. Encourage the children to say which of their choices are the same and which are different. Talk about how the items vary in appearance and use. For

example, two cups are the same because you drink from them, but the saucer is different because you put the cup on it. However, a cup and saucer may be the same because they are blue and the other cup different because it is red.

Now ask, *'How many things can we find that are different?'* Talk about the **shape**, **colour** and **size**. Put the items back and the next person has a turn.

> use
> pondering
> take your
> time

Number train

(Standing)

All walk around in a big circle counting, and end with a steam train noise:

> One, two, three, four, five, Whoo Whoo,
> One, two, three, four, five, Whoo Whoo...

> **relax and
> have fun**

Same-length ribbons

(Sitting)

Lay out two pieces of ribbon of the same length (or strips of card). Encourage the children to compare them and to see if they are the same or different in length. Involve all the children in this.

Then sit back and say that you are going to play a guessing game.

Lay out *identical* objects on one of the ribbons (e.g. same-size buttons, counters). Count with the group the number of objects on the ribbons. Now ponder how many things you can lay out on the other ribbon. Ponder aloud about the ribbons being the same length. *'Maybe you can get the same number of things on it. Mmm... That's true – how many things* [e.g. buttons] *will I put on it?'* Explore this with the group.

Closing round – Number hops

(Standing)

When you say *'one hop'* everyone does one hop, when you say *'two hops'* everyone does two hops. Then change to when you say *'one jump'* everyone does one jump, when you say *'two jumps'* everyone does two jumps and so on around the circle.

44

Session 10

Materials

- Large square of material (e.g. table cloth).
- A little plastic bottle or pot for each child in the group plus one extra (small yoghurt pots are ideal for this).
- Spotty dog mask and dotted cards with numerals on one side (one card for each person in the group).
- Toy animal.
- One set of coloured cards in pairs: two red, two blue, two green, and so on (one card for each person).
- Two plates (plastic or paper).
- Pile of stones.
- Pile of feathers.

Nearly there

(Standing)

Place a green shape at your feet. Tell a simple story about two animals who try to jump on to the shape. Choose two children to play the part of the animals. Place a red shape on the floor as a starting point. Give a toy animal to the two children to hold. Ask them to take turns making one jump at a time. Use the word 'nearly' as in nearly there: *'The rabbit is nearly there.'*

Afterwards see if anyone can remember how many jumps each animal made. Ponder with the children about why the jumps may have been different.

Big square shapes

(Sitting)

Bring out the large square of material and lay it out on the floor in the middle of the circle. Ask what shape it is, then ask individual children to:

- Walk around the sides and tell you how many sides there are. Ask, *'Can you slide your feet along a side?'*
- Stand on a corner.
- Hop along one side.
- Find a corner; now walk across the square to another corner in a diagonal line (where appropriate, demonstrate 'on', 'along', 'across').

Experiment folding the cloth by pulling one corner to another and ponder on the different shape you can make (triangle). Emphasise word **different** (i.e. it is not the same) with a slight shake of the head, saying, *'It's not the same'*, then, *'It's different.'*

End with a triangle. Ask, *'Has it got four sides? No? It can't be a square, it's changed, its different.'* Identify with the group that it has three sides so it must be a triangle.

Heavy and light

(Sitting)

Sit in a circle and pass around the plate of feathers saying, *'This is light.'* Then pass around the plate of stones and say, *'This is heavy.'* Comment on how different they feel.

Put the plates in the middle of the circle and invite the children one by one to pick up each one and say which is heavy and which is light.

**use
pondering
take your
time**

Matching pairs

(Sitting and standing)

From a set of coloured cards, select pairs of cards. Mix these up (shuffle), then hand them out – one card to each person in the group. The task is for each person to find the matching card. Say *'Go'* and everyone goes out to find their matching partner and stands beside them.

Sit down and count how many cards there are **altogether**. Then count how many there are of each colour.

Closing round – Number hops

(Standing)

When you say *'one hop'* everyone does one hop, when you say *'two hops'* everyone does two hops. Then change to when you say *'one jump'* everyone does one jump, when you say *'two jumps'* everyone does two jumps and so on around the circle.

Session 11

Materials

- Feely bag with two ribbons – one long and one short – and a toy animal.
- Ice-cream cut-outs individually from the resources page (you could use large counters and call them biscuits!).
- A jar of small plastic animals, approximately three to four for each person in the group.
- Number cards zero to eight in numerals (one for each person in the group).
- Toy animal.
- Tambourine.

Jumping game

(Standing)

Stand in a circle. Say that when you say the number **two** everyone must crouch down and when you say **five** they jump high in the air. Say this in a series of numbers: *zero, one, **two**, three, four, **five**, six, seven, eight, nine, ten, then nine, eight, seven, six, **five**, four, three, **two**, one, zero* (simplify as necessary).

```
relax and
have fun
```

Long tail and short tail

(Sitting)

Take from a feely bag two different lengths of ribbon, one long and one short. Discuss which one is long and which one is short. Pass the two ribbons around the group for the children to decide.

Then lay the ribbons out on the floor. Introduce a toy animal say, *'I am going to put my rabbit on a ribbon. Shall I choose the long ribbon* [ponder] *or the short ribbon? Mmm, I am going to put my rabbit on the short ribbon.'* Do this then pick the animal up and give it to a child. Ask them to say whether they are going to put the animal on the long or short ribbon before they act.

```
use
pondering
take your
time
```

Number hops

(Standing)

Pass the tambourine around for everyone to shake. Then say that you will beat the tambourine one, two or three times and name an action for each (e.g. when you give one beat say *'altogether one hop'* and everyone does one hop, when you say *'two hops'* everyone does two hops. Then change to *'one jump'* and everyone does one jump, when you say *'two jumps'* everyone does two jumps and so on around the circle. Then choose individuals by name (e.g. *'Alexandra, can you do three hops?'*).

Ice-creams for everyone

(Sitting. Use coloured counters as biscuits if ice-creams are not available)

Pass around a jar containing lots of small toy animals and ask everyone to take out a handful. Then use the cut-out ice-creams. Tell a story about the ice-cream man who comes into the woods to sell ice-creams to the animals.

Say, *'I've got three animals. I will need three ice-creams'* and take three ice-creams.

Ask each person in the circle, *'How many animals have you got?'* and *'How many ice-creams will you need?'*

Encourage the children to choose the number of ice-creams corresponding to what they say. This will help with checking one-to-one correspondence and use of language for number.

**use
pondering
take your
time**

Circle train with numbers

(Standing)

Randomly assign number cards (one to eight or number in the group) to people in the circle. Choose someone to be the engine. The task for the engine is to sort the carriages in order of number before the train can chug around the room. Ponder and ask, *'Who is first in the line? Who is next? Who is last?'* to the tune of *Here We Go Round the Mulberry Bush.*

Teddie is the first in line, first in line, first in line,
Teddie is the first in line on our train.
Wendy is the last in line, last in line, last in line,
Wendy is the last in line on our train.

**relax and
have fun**

Finding Numbers

(Sitting)

Lay out numbers one, two, three, four, five. Ask a child to stand on number four, then to sit down. Ask a child to stand on number one, then to sit down. Give each person in the circle a turn to find and stand on a number.

Then ask child (a) to tell child (b) to find a number for them to stand on. Give turns around the circle to encourage the **use** of language.

Closing round – Numbers

(Standing)

Each person says a number in sequence around the circle: one, two, three, four, five, six, seven and so on. Then try to reverse the sequence.

BE
POSITIVE

49

Session 12

Materials

- Feely bag containing three ribbons of different lengths.
- One toy animal.
- Set of numbered cards with dots inside the numbers. Two of each number for matching game.
- Large circle of material.
- Cut-out fish.

Animal tails (length)

(Sitting. Using vocabulary – short and long)

Draw out of a feely bag three ribbons of different lengths. Involve the children in deciding which is the shorter and which the longer. Lay the three ribbons out on the floor. Pass around the toy animal and invite children to say which ribbon they would choose to sit their animal on, using description of length to decide their decision (e.g. *'I will put my rabbit on the long ribbon.'*) Then ask another person in the circle, *'Which one will you put your animal on – short, long or longest?'*

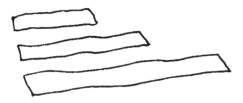

**use
pondering
take your
time**

Same as me game

(Standing)

All stand round in a circle and say, *'Watch me. I'm going to put my hands behind my back. Can you do the same as me?'*

  Perform a series of actions, encouraging the children to imitate the same actions (pat head, hop, turn around). Emphasise the phrase **Same as me**.

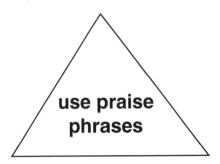

**use praise
phrases**

Matching pairs

(Sitting, then standing)

From a set of matching number cards give a card to each child. Tell them they will be looking for someone with the same numbered card as theirs. Just before you begin the game ask each child to tell you how many spots they have on their card and to hold the card out in front of them. All find a pair. Praise the group and sit back in the circle ready for the next game.

Big circle shape

(Sitting)

Bring out the large circle of materials and lay it on the floor in the middle of the group. Ask what shape it is, then choose individual children to walk carefully around the circle. Talk about why there are no corners. Then walk across the shape.

Experiment by folding the cloth in half to make a **semicircle**, then choose children to walk along the sides – explore the changes. Discuss with the children about corners and sides.

Put the cloth back into the original position. Look at it together, see that the corners and the straight side have gone, then refold it into a semicircular shape. Give it the name **semicircle**. Explain that it is **half a circle**.

Talk about the face. Ponder that you can see only a bit of the face when the cloth is folded. Ponder that it looks **different**. You have changed the shape. Choose a child to stand on the cloth. Ask them, *'Do you want a circle or a semicircle?'* Encourage the child to say the word **before** they make the shape. Then allow them to lay out the cloth in the shape they have chosen and then to stand on the cloth. Then ask, *'Tanya, what shape are you standing on?'*

use pondering take your time

Nearly there

(Standing)

Place a green shape at your feet. Tell a simple story about two animals who try to jump on to the shape. Choose two children to play the part of the animals. Place a red shape on the floor as a starting point. Give a toy animal to each of the two children to hold. Ask the children to take turns making one jump at a time. Use the word 'nearly' as in nearly there: *'The rabbit is nearly there.'*

Now play the game again but choose one child. Ask them to move towards the green shape and add instructions to move fast or slowly. For example, *'Walk slowly.' 'Jump quickly.'*

Half and half

(Sitting)

Lay out six objects; two animals have to have half each. The group helps them to work this out.

Closing round – Number song

(Standing)

Hold up the cut-out fish and tell the group, *'You are going to sing a song about catching a fish'.* Sing *'One, two, three, four, five, once I caught a fish alive.'*

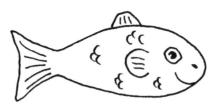

Hold up the fish and say, *'And I give the fish to George.'*

Then we all sing *'One, two, three, four, five, once I caught a fish alive.'* George holds up the fish and says *'And I give the fish to Marmee.'*

And so on until all the children have had a turn.

> **relax and
> have fun**

Session 13

Materials

- Interesting box containing a number three cut-out.
- Feely bag.
- Large number three cut out of a large piece of cloth or paper.
- Three plates – one with a building brick (plastic or wood) on, one with a pile of stones on and one with feathers on.
- Large square cloth.
- King and hedgehog puppets.

Number box

(Sitting)

Bring out the interesting box. Say, *'I've got a number in my box – can you guess what it is?'*

Allow the children to guess. Then say, *'I'll give you a clue.'* Show them the card with three spots and say, *'This tells us what the number is.'* Take guesses: *'It's number three!'*

Take the number three out of the feely bag. Model running your finger around it saying *'three'.* Pass it around the circle for each child to do the same. Then ask each child to carry out an action involving three (e.g. give three nods, three claps, show three fingers and so on). Ask, *'How many did you do?'*

> use
> pondering
> take your
> time

Big number shape

(Sitting)

Lay out a large number three cut out from a large piece of cloth or paper. Encourage children one by one to walk along the number. Ponder that depending where you are sitting on the circle the number three can look different. Ask two children sitting opposite each other in the circle to look carefully at the number and then to change places and look again to see if it looks different. Ask them to decide which is the **right way up**. Decide which is the top of the number and put a mark of some sort on the top of the number. As a group, hold hands and walk around the circle and see how the number appears to change shape.

Put the shape away.

Heaviest and lightest

(Sitting)

Lay out in the circle a plate with one wooden brick, a plate with one stone and a plate with one feather on it. Invite the children to guess first which plate will be the lightest or the heaviest and then to test their estimates by picking up the plate of their choice (make sure that the brick/stone are not too similar in weight).

Shape game

(Standing and singing)

Song to the tune of *Here We Go Gathering Nuts In May*.

Lay out a large square cloth. Talk briefly about the shape, corners and sides. Then ask the group to walk round the sides singing:

> We are walking round the sides
> Round the sides, round the sides.
> We are walking round the sides,
> Round the sides of the square.

Then all sit down. Ask the children to decide whether the sides are the same or if some sides are longer.

Say, *'Let's see if we can make a rectangle, but let's ask the King and the hedgehog to help us.'*

Bring in the hedgehog who asks, *'What is a rectangle?'* Explore this with the children.

The hedgehog then ponders, *'Oh, so a rectangle has two long sides and two short sides.'*

Get the hedgehog to hide his eyes. Choose a child to fold the cloth into a rectangular shape. Decide as a group what the shape is called, then ask the hedgehog to open his eyes and say what shape it is.

Do this several times, making either a rectangle or a square with the cloth. Each time use the descriptions:

- Two long sides and two short sides for a rectangle.
- Four sides all the same for a square.

Allow the hedgehog to make mistakes to enable the children to help him out. Then after a while bring out the King who tests the hedgehog on his knowledge of shapes.

One last question the King should ask: *'How do you know those sides are longer?'* Ask the group how they could check and explore this.

Then pass the hedgehog around for a hug. Carefully put both King and hedgehog away.

> **use**
> **pondering**
> **take your**
> **time**

Closing game – Same as me

(Sitting)

Ask the group look at you while you hold up three fingers. Say the name of someone in the group and ask them to hold up the same as you and then tell you how many fingers they are holding up. They then have to hold up their fingers and ask someone else to count them. For example, *'Deepak – how many fingers am I holding up?'* Deepak replies with the correct number, then he holds up (e.g. four fingers) and asks Peter: *'Peter – how many fingers am I holding up?'*

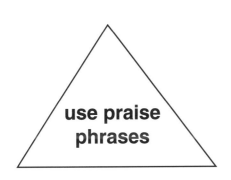

Session 14

Materials
- Large soft ball.
- Large rectangular cloth (table cloth or remnant).
- Six toy animals of different heights.
- Divided dots/numerals on cards – one per person in the group.

Roll the ball and count

(Sitting)

Roll the ball to someone in the circle and say *'one'*. They roll it to someone else and say *'two'* and so on. Ensure that everyone has a turn.

Big shapes changing

(Sitting and standing)

Lay out a large piece of rectangular cloth. Identify the shape with the group. Ask children to walk along the sides and count them. Next demonstrate walking along a side and stopping at the corners. Count as you go the sides and corners. Then all walk along the sides of the cloth, singing (to the tune of *Here We Go Round the Mulberry Bush*):

> We are walking round the sides, round the sides, round the sides,
> We are walking round the sides, the rectangle has four sides.

Next tell the group to find the corners and each to stand on one corner. Sing as above but change to:

> We are jumping on the corners, on the corners, on the corners;
> We are jumping on the corners, the rectangle has four corners.

Ask the children to stand on a long side of the rectangle and sing:

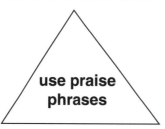

> We are standing on the long side, on the long side, on the long side;
> We are standing on the long side, the rectangle has got two long sides.

Do the same with the short sides. Then all sit down. Invite children, individually, to walk, hop, skip and jump along the sides and from corner to corner. **Ask each person to tell you how he or she will move and where before he or she begins.**

use praise
phrases

Size order

(Sitting)

Three animals are quarrelling about who is the biggest. Ask the children to sort the animals into size order as a group. Ask on behalf of the animals how the children decided. Talk to them about which is the largest/tallest/smallest.

More animals

(Sitting)

Talk about **adding** some **more** animals to sort. Bring out three more animals and ask the group to re-sort using all six.

Circle train with numbers

(Standing)

Randomly assign number cards (one to eight or number in the group) to people in the circle. Choose someone to be the engine. The task for the engine is to sort the carriages in order of number before the train can chug around the room. Ponder and ask, *'Who is first in the line? Who is next? Who is last?'* to the tune of *Here We Go Round the Mulberry Bush.*

> Linda is the first in line, first in line, first in line
> Linda is the first in line on our train.
> David is the last in line, last in line, last in line,
> David is the last in line on our train

Half and half

(Sitting)

Lay out six objects. Two animals have to have half each (equal amounts). The group helps them to work this out.

BE POSITIVE

Closing round – Counting down

(Standing)

Each person calls out one number in sequence; then reverse the numbers so that you are counting back down.

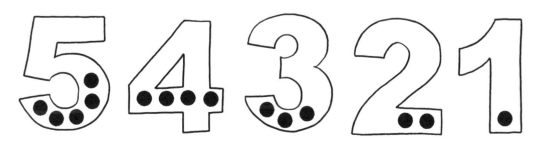

Session 15

Materials

- Large square cloth.
- Interesting box containing a triangle shape and a square shape.
- Three triangles.
- Three ribbons of different lengths.
- Spotty dog pictures.
- Dotted/numbered cards.
- Red and blue circles, enough for each child to have one each.

Growing numbers

(Active)

All crouch on the floor.

Count 'one, two, three, four, and five', as you all get taller. Then stretch your arms right up when you get to five. All clap hands and jump once.

Spotty dog

(Standing)

One of the adults holds the spotty dog picture and dog without spots. The dog has to collect his spots. He needs to collect one spot first then his spots from the head down towards the tail. Ask, *'Who has got one spot? Come and wear the spotty dog mask. Who has got two spots?... come and stand behind...'* and so on, making a line to represent the spotty dog. Encourage the children to identify this by themselves. Children with more spots are at the 'tail end' – as in the picture.

When *everyone* is in the line:

Ask which person is **first** and which person **last** – who has a few spots – as the front/head of the dog, who has more spots – as the tail end of the dog.

Then act out a little story together of the dog sniffing through the grass wagging his tail (hands behind their backs). He yawns and stretches, and curls up to have a sleep.

use
pondering
take your
time

Big shapes changing

(Sitting)

Lay out the large square cloth in the middle of the circle. Ask a child to find and stand on a corner, then to pick up the corner and walk over to another corner, folding the cloth as they go.

Depending on which corners are chosen, the shape will be a triangle or a rectangle.

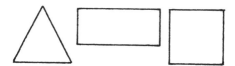

Ask who can tell what the new shape is. Choose children to tell you whether they will walk along the sides or count the corners.

Choose children to take a turn folding the cloth. Encourage them to **tell** you whether they are going to make a rectangle or a triangle in advance. When a triangle is made ask the children if all the sides are the same length. Ask for ideas on how you can check this.

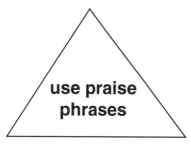

What's in my box?

(Sitting)

Say that there are two shapes in your box and you want the children to guess what they are. Encourage them to think of questions they could ask (e.g. *'How many sides does it have? How many corners does it have? Are all the sides the same?'*). Encourage children to use the language.

Number train

(Standing)

All walk around in a big circle counting, and end with steam train noise:

One, two, three, four, five, Whoo, Whoo
One, two, three, four, five, Whoo Whoo...

Animal's ribbons

(Sitting)

Three animals have a ribbon each. Help them to decide which has the longest ribbon and which has the shortest and put in order of length.

Closing round – Patterns

(Sitting in a semicircle to leave a space for children to line up)

Place red and blue circles in a group on the floor in front of you. Ask one child to choose a colour and to stand up in the space in the circle.

Then ask another child to take a colour and stand next to the first child. Talk about the pattern they are making (e.g. it may be red, blue, red, red, and blue, red). Talk again about the pattern. Ask each child what colour will be next. Ask the next child to choose that colour and stand in the line in the right place. Encourage the children to complete a pattern. Go back into a circle and do a round, with each child saying the name of a colour in the sequence out loud.

Keep a note of the pattern for a future session.

use
pondering
take your
time

Session 16

┌───┐
Materials
* One large object and one small object to pass around.
* Number cards – one for each person in the group.
* King and hedgehog puppets.
* Big round cloth or circle of paper.
* Number box with numerals three and four.
* A circle for each person in the group.
└───┘

Opening round

(Standing)

Each person holds a number card facing outwards. Count around the group, then count around again, with each person sitting down when their number is called out.

Big round cloth with King and hedgehog

(Sitting)

Lay the big round cloth on the floor. Talk about having one long curved side or edge. All walk around the circle singing (to the tune of *Here We Go Round the Mulberry Bush*):

> The round shape has one long curved side, one long curved side, one long curved side,
> The round shape has one long curved side all around it. It goes all around it.

Bring out the King and the hedgehog. The King asks the hedgehog to find the corners. The hedgehog shows that he is puzzled and asks the children for help. He tells the King that he can't find any corners on the round shape. The King laughs kindly and says that it was just a little joke, the round shape hasn't got any corners.

The hedgehog says *'Oh, the King is teasing me. There are no corners on the round shape'*.

The King asks the hedgehog if he can think of a shape that does have corners? Involve the children in helping the hedgehog in finding an answer. Then put the puppets away carefully and all sit down.

┌──────────────┐
**use
pondering
take your
time**
└──────────────┘

One more sitting

(Sitting)

Each person in the group has a circle. Put yours on the floor and say, *'I want one more. Niamh, can you give me one more?'* As each person gives you a circle lay it on the floor in front of you.

Same and different actions

(Sitting and standing)

Ask three people to stand in the middle of the circle. Ask them to jump up and down several times, then stop them and tell two of them that they will be jumping next and the other person will be doing froggie-hops. Start all three off. Then ask the rest of the children who is doing the **same** and who is doing something **different**. Choose three more people, then repeat. Do this a third time to allow everyone to have a turn to be in an active group of three at least once.

My number box three and four

(Sitting)

Say, *'I have a number in my box. It is one more than two.'*

Ask the group for ideas as to how to find out what the number is. Then put out a handful of bricks. Encourage the children to work out their ideas. Help where needed so that they eventually put out two bricks, then add one more to get three. Take out and then show the numeral three. Pass it around the circle to each person. Talk about three being more than two.

Repeat, saying, *'I have another number in my box. It is one more than three.'*

Ask the group for ideas. Encourage use of bricks to check their answers. Then show the numeral four. Model holding it and exploring the shape. Pass it around the circle to each person. Talk about the shape.

Ponder that number four looks different to number three.

Show them how to draw a number three in the air (make sure they are behind you for this, otherwise they see a mirror image). Get the children to draw a three in the air – starting at the top. Watch to see that they go in the right direction. Ask them to draw a three on each others' backs. Repeat for number four.

> use
> pondering
> take your
> time

Closing round – Big thing small thing

(Sitting)

Pass a small object around the circle, saying, *'This is a small thing.'*
Pass a large object around the circle, saying, *'This is a big thing.'*

Session 17

Materials

- Dotted/numeral cards.
- Same-sized square for each person in the group.
- Cube with a stick-on face on each face of the cube.
- Five toy animals.
- Cards zero, one, two, three.
- Tambourine.

Opening round – Dotty hops

(Standing)

Give out dotted numeral cards in random order. Say, *'We are going to take turns. If you have number one do one hop, if you have number two do two hops, three hops'* and so on. Encourage children to participate as their number is called out. Do this twice, then, instead of saying the number, beat it out on the tambourine. Give the children the opportunity to take turns.

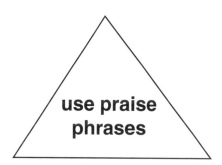

use praise phrases

Comparing squares and cubes

(Sitting)

Hand out the same-sized squares, one for each person. Then take out a cube (brick). Ponder that it has a square on the bottom, a square on the top and squares round the sides. Demonstrate each point by running your finger and hand over the cube while you talk about it. Explain that these are called 'faces'. Count the faces with the group. Say it is a solid shape and give the name **Cube**. Pass it around the group, asking children to see how many faces they can count on the cube.

Faces on a cube

(Sitting)

Lay out the stick-on faces in a row and count them with the group.

Say, *'Let's see how many faces there are on the cube. Let's use these paper faces and stick them on the cube, counting as we go.'*

Stick and count the faces on each face of the cube, encouraging the children to call out the numbers with you. Then pass the cube with the faces around the group so that each person can check.

> **use pondering take your time**

Zero meanies

(Sitting)

Give cards zero, one, two and three to the four toy animals. Choose children individually to take one, two or three small objects from a jar next to you and to give it to the right animal with the corresponding card (after a while the animal with the zero card complains that he hasn't got any).

Talk about zero meaning nothing.

Number train with choosing

(Standing)

Choose a child to be an engine and give them a card with the 'zero' on it. Talk about this being zero or nought or nothing, and that it is a good point from which to start.

Give out the number cards (use dotted/numeral cards if still needed by some of the group).

The task of the engine is to collect and sort the carriages into the correct number order. Then all chug around in a big circle counting and ending with steam train noise:

One, two, three, four, five, Whoo Whoo,
One, two, three, four, five, Whoo Whoo...

> **relax and have fun**

I'm the biggest animal

(Sitting)

Five animals quarrel about who is the biggest and who is the smallest. Engage the group in sorting out in size order which is the biggest and which is the smallest. Say, *'First is the mouse, he is the smallest, next is the cat, next'*, and so on. Then say, *'This one is last, he is the biggest.'*

Closing round – Same as me

(Standing)

All think of a number from zero to five. All hold up fingers to show which number they have chosen.

Say *'Go!'* and hold up that number of fingers. See how many people have chosen to hold up the same number of fingers as you.

Do this several times.

Ensure that zero is included somewhere in one of the turns. If you have children in the group who experience motor co-ordination difficulties you may wish to use markers instead of fingers for this game.

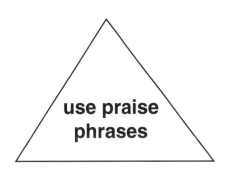

Session 18

Materials

- Square shape in a box.
- Spotty dog pictures and spot number cards.
- Dotted counting cards.
- Cube shape.
- Hedgehog puppet.
- Thick pen.

There is something in my box

(Sitting)

Say you have a shape in your box. Say it has four sides and four corners. When the group guesses *'square'*, gradually ease the shape from the box so that the children can see a bit at a time until you remove it from the box completely.

Say, *'Yes, you are right. It is a square.'*

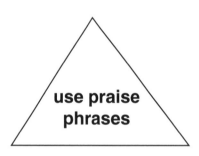

use praise phrases

Spotty dog

(Standing)

One of the adults holds the spotty dog picture and dog without spots. The dog has to collect his spots. He needs to collect one spot first then his spots from the head down towards the tail. Ask, *'Who has got one spot? Come and hold the picture of the spotty dog. Who has got two spots?...come and stand behind...'* and so on, making a line to represent the spotty dog. Encourage the children to identify this by themselves. Children with more spots are at the 'tail end' – as in the picture.

When *everyone* is in the line:

Ask which person is **first** and which person **last** – who has a few spots – as the front/head of the dog, who has more spots – as the tail end of the dog.

Then act out a little story together of the dog sniffing through the grass wagging his tail (hands behind their backs). He yawns and stretches, and curls up to have a sleep.

Solid shapes

(Sitting)

Talk about the last session when you looked at a cube. Show the cube with drawn or stick-on faces, one on each face of the cube. Count the faces.

Bring in the hedgehog. Explain that he needs help to remember that these flat bits are called faces and it helps him to draw faces on to each surface.

Place a large box in the middle of the circle. Ask the group to organise themselves so that six people stand up (e.g. choose one child to choose five other people).

Each person will either draw or stick on one face.

After they have done this, ponder that you have six people and they have all drawn one face each, so a cube must have six faces. Check this with the group.

Sing as a group to the tune *Here We Go Round the Mulberry Bush*:

> We put six faces on the cube, on the cube, on the cube,
> We put six faces on the cube so we know it has six faces.

Estimate number

(Sitting)

Place a number of small objects beside you. Talk about estimating being different from counting – it is a good guess. Tell a child to take as many objects as they can hold in one hand and then estimate how many they are holding. Pass them around the circle so that everyone gives an estimate.

Put the pile in the middle of the circle.

Then take another handful yourself and count them, and compare them visually with the first pile of objects, using the words **same as, look the same as, different, about the same, less than** and **more than**. Compare the piles visually only at this stage.

Ask how else you could check if they are the same (if a child mentions heavy/light, use this as a comparison too).

Closing round – Same as me

(Standing)

All think of a number from zero to five. All hold up fingers to show what number they have chosen.

Say *'Go!'* and hold up that number of fingers. See how many people have chosen to hold up the same number of fingers as you.

Do this several times. (Ensure that nought is included somewhere in one of the turns).

Session 19

Materials

- Circle shape in a box.
- Same-sized square for each person.
- A cube.
- Two animals.
- Balance scales.
- Dotted numeral cards.
- A shape for each person in the group – circle or triangle (all the same colour).

I have a shape in my box

(Sitting)

Say, *'It has no corners, and one long curved side.'* After the group have guessed, bring out the shape slowly. Stop and remark when it is a semicircle and then remove it from the box completely.

Making cubes from squares

(Sitting)

Hand out the same-sized squares, one for each person. Then take out a cube. Ponder that it has a square face on the bottom, a square face on the top and square faces round the sides. Demonstrate each face by running your finger and hand over the cube while you talk about it. Count the faces with the group. Give the name **Cube**. Pass it around the group, asking children to see how many faces they can count on the cube. Now ask the group how you can make the squares look like the cube.

Ponder on what has been achieved and praise for good thinking.

Same as me

(Standing)

All stand up in a circle and say, *'Watch me, I'm going to put my hands behind my back. Can you do the same as me?'*

Perform a series of actions, encouraging the children to imitate these same actions (pat head, hop, turn around). Emphasise the words **same as me**.

Heaviest, lightest animal

(Sitting)

Two animals quarrel about which is heaviest and
which is lightest. Discuss with the group ways of
deciding which is the heaviest and which is the
lightest. First invite children to estimate by holding
animals in each hand.

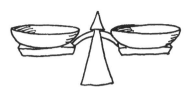

Then bring out the scales. Ask the children what they think will happen. Explain that
the lightest animal will be higher on the scales and the heaviest animal will be lower
on the scales. *'We call this **weighing the animals**. Then we will **weigh the animals**.
We will see which is the heaviest and which is the lightest.'*

Matching pairs

(Sitting, then standing)

From the two sets of matching spotted number cards give a card to each child. Tell
them they will be looking for someone with the same numbered card as theirs. Just
before you begin the game ask each child to tell you how many spots they have on
their card and to hold the card out in front of them. Then all find a pair. Praise the
group and sit back in the circle ready for the next game. Then say, *'number order'*, and
the pairs have to get in a line in their order of number (e.g. zero zero, one one, two
two).

Half and half

(Sitting)

Lay out six objects. Two animals have to have half
each. The group help them to work this out. Then
share a coloured sheet of paper between the two
animals. Help them to decide which is half.

> **use
> pondering
> take your
> time**

Closing round patterns

(Sitting in a semicircle to leave a space for children to line up)

Lay out the circles and triangles in front of you in a group. Say, *'We are going to make
a different pattern.'* Ask one child to choose a shape and to stand up in the space in
the circle. Talk about pattern very simply as a group.

Then ask another child to choose a shape and to stand next to the first child. Talk
about the pattern they are making (e.g. it may be circle, circle or triangle, triangle or
circle, triangle). Ask what shape is next. Talk again about the pattern. Ask each child
what shape will be next. Ask the next child to choose that shape and to stand in the
line in the right place. Encourage the children to complete a pattern. Go back into a
circle and do a round, with each child saying the name of their shape out loud.

Session 20

Materials

- Balance scales.
- Jar with small objects in.
- Dice.
- King and hedgehog puppets.
- Felt-tip pen and A3 square of paper.
- Cube-shaped cardboard box.
- Three fluffy animals.
- Various cardboard shapes (circle, semicircle, square, triangle, rectangle and star).

Speedy numbers

(Standing)

As quickly as possible count around the circle, with each person saying one number in sequence – zero, one, two, three, four, five, six, seven, eight, then reverse this to eight, seven, six, five, four, three, two, one and zero.

Lightest, heaviest

(Sitting)

Three animals argue about which is the lightest and which is the heaviest. The group help them to work this out. Talk about checking this using balance scales. Explain the effects that a heavier weight will have (e.g. a heavier weight will bring that side of the balance down). Then bring out the scales. Ask the children what they think will happen. Explain that the lightest animal will be higher on the scales and the heaviest animal will be lower on the scales. *'We call this **weighing the animals.** Then we will **weigh the animals.** We will see which is the heaviest and which is the lightest.'*

use
pondering
take your
time

Spotted dice – Good guessing

(Sitting)

Throw a spotted dice. Count how many spots are on the topmost face. One person in the group is then chosen to take a handful of small objects from a jar and lay them out in a line in front of them. The task is to count the objects and then to tell the group if they have enough or too many to cover the spots on top of the dice before checking this with one-to-one correspondence.

This decision is tested out by putting their objects one-to-one on the spots of the dice.

Talk about:

- Too many;
- One more;
- One less;
- One left over;
- Too few, not enough.

Each person throws a dice and takes a turn.

One more

(Standing)

Explain to the children that you are going to hold up one finger and the person next to you has to hold up one finger and then **one more** finger. Explore children's understanding of that. Go around the circle helping children to hold up **one more** finger than the person before. At the end count around the circle.

The hedgehog's test

(Sitting)

Bring out the King and the hedgehog. Say it's the hedgehog's test! The King asks questions but says that the hedgehog can ask people for help.

The hedgehog asks the people to put their hands up and he will choose someone to help him.

If a child gives a wrong answer, the hedgehog says, *'Thank you. I think I will get some more ideas. Who can I choose?'*

The child who has given the wrong answer to the hedgehog can help to choose someone else for more ideas.

The King's questions are:

- Can you find me a circle, a semicircle, a square, a triangle, a rectangle, and a star?
- Show, one by one, a circle, a semicircle, a square, a triangle, a rectangle and a star and ask what these shapes are called.

Lay out the shapes in a row and select them one by one to ask the children the following questions:

- How many sides does each have?
- How many corners does each have?

Put away these shapes. Then ask:

- How many faces does a cube have? Take ideas.

Bring out a large cubed cardboard box with a lid, having marked a 'face' on each face of the cube. Open out the flattened box. The hedgehog gets very involved in counting the faces. He invites the children to join in, getting a child to stand on each face, then counting the children.

The hedgehog says, *'Even though they haven't got faces drawn on them they are still called faces.'*

Make up the box again with the hedgehog *inside* it. The King comes along and asks, *'Where is the hedgehog?'*

He looks on **top**, **around**, **behind** and **underneath** the box. A muffled squeal comes from the box: *'I'm stuck **inside** the box. Let me out.'*

The hedgehog is helped out of the box.

'I didn't like being inside a cube', he says.

Pass him around for a hug and put the hedgehog and the King away.

Closing round – Do the same and different from me

(Standing)

Ask the children to do the same as you:

- Touch your nose.
- Put your hands behind your back.
- Hop . . . and so on.

Choose one of the children to be the leader.

Ask the children to perform some action different from you:

- Touch your nose
- Put your hands behind your back
- Hop . . . and so on

Choose one of the children to be the leader.

relax and have fun

Session 21

Materials

- Wooden or plastic circles (enough for one per person in the group).
- Cylinder shape (may be unopened tin or packet).
- Cardboard tubes (kitchen paper or toilet roll tubes).
- Clean paper and pencil.
- Three cube-shaped objects for each person in the group plus one more.
- A set of matching number cards, zero zero, one one, two two and so on.
- Toy bear.

Drawing shapes and guessing

(Sitting)

On a piece of paper in front of you draw a shape slowly. Ask the children to stop you and guess when they think they know what shape you are drawing. Give a couple of turns to each child.

Don't do the same as me

(Standing)

Instead of asking children to do the same as you, tell them they must do something different:

- So that when you touch your nose they must perform a different action.
- Put your hands behind your back.
- Hop . . . and so on.

Emphasise the word different.

Choose one of the children to be the leader to continue the game.

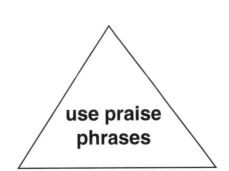

use praise
phrases

73

Circles to cylinders

(Sitting)

Take out a solid shape, a cylinder, from a box (e.g. an unopened tin can or carton). Ponder as it is passed around that it has circles at both ends and it has a smooth curved face all the way around. Emphasise this by running your finger over it. Pass it around so that the children can run their fingers over it. Talk about the two round faces, one at each end.

Hand out same-size circles to each person in the group and place cardboard tubes in the middle.

Ask the group how they could make their own cylinders.

Encourage problem-solving to achieve this. Praise good thinking and putting forward good ideas to try.

**use
pondering
take your
time**

Have you enough for Mr Bear?

(Sitting)

Give each person in the group two cubes, but give one person an extra one so that they have three cubes.

Introduce a bear that will ask them to help him by giving him the number of cubes that he asks for.

The bear then asks each person around the circle:

'Can you give me three cubes? Have you enough?'

Each person tells Mr Bear how many they have and whether they have enough to give him three cubes. Then the person who has three cubes gives Mr Bear their cubes and changes places with him. Mr Bear gives them back their cubes, saying, *'Mr Bear wants everyone to have **one more**'.*

He ponders lightly and briefly: *'How many will you each have then?'*

Ask the group for thoughts and ideas.

Mr Bear then gives one more cube to each person, saying, *'Here is one more. If I give you this how many will you have?'*

When everyone in the group has one extra cube he asks: *'Can you give me four cubes. Have you enough?'*

By this time only the person who had three cubes last time will have enough, so they change places with Mr Bear again.

Ponder why this is so, and talk about three and **one more** being four. The rest of the group all have **one less**, so they have three.

Mr Bear thanks the group and wonders aloud: *'How many cubes are there* ***altogether****?'* He suggests that all the cubes are put in the middle of the circle and that the children help him to count how many cubes there are. The cubes are then put away.

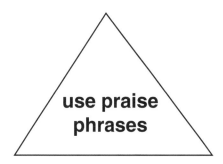

Closing round – Find your number pair

(Standing)

Give a card from the set of matching number cards to each child. Tell them they will be looking for someone with the same numbered card as theirs. Just before you begin the game, ask each child to tell you how many spots they have on their card and to hold the card out in front of them. All find a pair. Praise the group and sit back in the circle ready for the next game. Then say, *'number order'*, and the pairs have to stand in a line in their order of number (e.g. zero zero, one one, two two).

Session 22

```
┌─────────────────────────────────────────────────────────────┐
│                        Materials                             │
│  • Number cards.                                             │
│  • Ten objects to arrange into piles.                       │
│  • Weasel and bear.                                          │
│  • Four toy animals.                                         │
│  • Jar containing objects.                                   │
│  • Two triangles – one regular with equal sides, one         │
│    irregular with one side longer.                          │
└─────────────────────────────────────────────────────────────┘
```

Number train

(Standing)

Hand out number cards in random order. Choose an 'engine' that invites children by number or to be the carriages of the train. Ask: *'Who is third? Who is before Ellen? Who is after Sandeep?'* Before you begin, encourage the children to check that the train is in the right number order and then chug around the room.

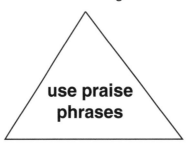

use praise phrases

Mr Bear's missing number game

(Sitting)

Mr Bear puts out piles of objects numbering between one and four. He counts them and emphasises that they are in number order. He asks the children to watch them for him and goes behind the adult's back.

Enter the mischievous weasel that looks at the piles of objects, chooses pile three, takes away the objects and hides them under the box. He then moves the remaining piles of objects to change their order.

Mr Bear comes back and notices that one pile of objects is missing. Mr Weasel says that he will give the things back if Mr Bear can guess which pile is missing, but warns that if he gets it wrong he won't!

Mr Bear asks the children if they know which pile it is and how he can check how many were in that pile.

With the group, problem-solve ways to check this by putting the piles back in number order and seeing which pile is missing. Encourage strategies such as choosing one person to represent each number from one to four, getting them to line up in order, then to retrieve their pile of objects.

When the correct one is identified the mischievous weasel gives the pile back.

use
pondering
take your
time

Zero meanies

(Sitting)

Give cards zero, one, two and three to the four toy animals. Choose children individually to take one, two or three small objects from a jar next to you and give it to the right animal with the corresponding card (after a while the animal with the zero card complains that he hasn't got any).

Talk about zero meaning nothing.

Number train with choosing

(Standing)

Choose an 'engine' to give a card with the 'zero'. Talk about this being zero or nought or nothing, and that it is a good point from which to start.

Give out the number cards (use dotted/numeral card if still needed by some of the group)

The task of the engine is to collect the carriages in the correct number order. Then all chug around in a big circle counting and ending with steam train noise.

One, two, three, four, five, Whoo whoo,
One, two, three, four, five, Whoo whoo.

relax and
have fun

Different triangles

(Sitting)

Lay out two different triangles (one regular, one irregular). Talk about them both being triangles. Count the sides. Find out if all the sides are the same length on the regular triangle. Ask for ideas as to how you could do that (e.g. stepping along it, measuring with fingers). Using the irregular triangle, take estimates as to which is the longest side then use children's ideas as to how you could check this.

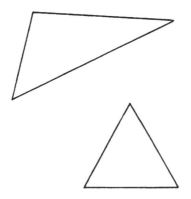

Closing round – Same as me, different from me

(Standing)

Ask the group to look at you while you hold up three fingers. Say the name of someone in the group and ask them to hold up the same fingers as you and then to tell you how many fingers they are holding up. They then have to hold up their fingers and ask someone else to count them (e.g. *'Damian – how many fingers am I holding up?'*). Damian replies with the correct number, then he holds up (e.g. four fingers) and asks Peter: *'Peter – how many fingers am I holding up?'*

Then, instead of asking the children to do the same as you, tell them they must do something different:

- So that when you touch your nose they must do a different action.
- Put your hands behind your back.
- Hop . . . and so on.

Emphasise the word **different**.

Choose one of the children to be the leader to continue the game.

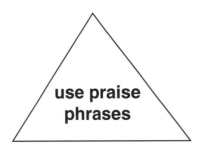

Session 23

Materials

- Number cards.
- Three cloth shapes to hide wooden shapes underneath.
- Red and blue wooden or plastic shapes, one for each person in the group (e.g. rectangle, star, circle, triangle and square).
- King and hedgehog puppets.
- Two yellow hoops.
- Jar of objects.
- Toy animals.

Counting in twos

(Standing)

Hand out a number card to each person in the group in sequence (the even numbers are printed or coloured-in in a different colour). Say that you are going to count in twos, then point to everyone but only *say* the even numbers (e.g. point silently/point and say two/point silently/point and say four).

Explain that the numbers two, four, six and eight are called even numbers. Ponder lightly and briefly as to why this may be.

Encourage the group to do this themselves by prompting only those children holding an even number card to say their number. Go round several times.

Then ask the group to tell you which numbers you *didn't* say. Ask the even numbers to sit down, then read out the odd numbers and say that the even numbers are sitting down so that those standing up have **odd numbers**.

Hedgehog's shape treasure hunt

(Sitting)

Tell the children that you are going to be helping the King to hide some shapes so that the hedgehog can have a treasure hunt which means that he will collect as many shapes as he can.

Lay out in the middle of the circle the three cloths – triangular, circular and square. Ask the King to choose individual children to show him a wooden shape and say that if they can tell you what shape it is they can tell you under which cloth to hide it. Encourage the children to tell you under which cloth they want you to hide the shape. It is important at this point to stimulate use of the language.

The children then tell the King which cloth they would like the shape hidden under.

Once all the shapes are hidden, bring in the hedgehog. He is quite excited about playing the game.

He says, *'I would like to find a nice circle. Can you give me clues so that I will know where to look?'*

The King asks, *'What types of clue would you like?'*

The hedgehog replies, *'Well, if you would say things like the circle treasure is under a cloth with three sides and three corners then I will know that I will need to look under the triangle cloth.'*

Help the hedgehog to find the shapes that he chooses by describing the properties of the cloth under which each is hidden. Involve the children in this as much as possible.

Making up groups

(Standing)

Put out two yellow hoops. Hand around the red and blue shapes. Invite the children to form into two groups standing in the hoops. Ask the children to give you ideas about what groups you could make (e.g. a red group and a blue group).

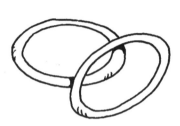

When the children have identified these two groups, bring them back into the circle again and ask if there are any other ways they could make two groups (e.g. squares and triangles).

Tell me one more

(Sitting)

Place your jar of objects beside you. Put the two toy animals in the middle of the circle with an object in front of them. Invite children individually to take one object from your jar and to tell you which animal they will give 'one more' to and how many that animal will have then.

Use the term 'one more', frequently commenting that *'Two is one more than one'*, *'Three is one more than two'* and so on.

Closing round – Point and count

(Standing)

Give each person around the circle a number and point to each person in turn, saying, *'One hop, two hop, three hop'* and so on until everyone in the group is hopping. Then point in reverse order, saying, *'Four stop, three stop, two stop, one stop.'* At the end pass a smile around the circle.

BE
POSITIVE

Session 24

Materials

- Large cloth.
- Addy the Adder (a little snake puppet with a plus sign on her back can be made with a sock pulled over your hand).
- Hedgehog and King puppets.
- Solid cube shape and flat square shape.
- Number cards, one for each person in the group.

Time to sing

(Sitting, then standing)

Talk to the group about what they did this morning **before** they came to school. Select five of these activities and put them into a little chant as follows:

> This morning I got out of bed,
> This morning I brushed my teeth,
> This morning I washed my hands,
> This morning I put on my clothes,
> And then I had my breakfast.

Chorus:

> That's what we do in the morning.

Stand up with the group and sing this together.

Addy the Adder

(Standing)

The children sit in a circle with a large cloth in the middle. Introduce a little snake called Addy, who is an adder. Addy adds things all the time. She makes them more.

Addy then chooses people in the group, one by one, to stand on the cloth in the middle of the circle. Each time Addy says, *'I'm going to add one more person'*, and chooses one person from the group to join the person(s) in the middle. Ask the group each time to say how many people there are in the middle now.

When everyone apart from you is in the middle, Addy the Adder says she is going to go home now and says goodbye to everyone.

Say that you want to see how many people are in the group. Ask them to stand in a line and count them. Then sit down ready for the next game.

Hedgehog hunts the coin shapes

(Sitting)

Place the solid cube shape and the flat square shape in the circle. Say that the King will hide a coin under one of them and the hedgehog has to guess which one it is. The hedgehog hides his eyes while the coin is placed under one of the shapes. For the first turn help the hedgehog by asking the children the following questions:

'Is it under a solid shape or a flat shape?'

Then:

'What is the shape called?'

Counting in twos

(Standing and sitting)

Ask the group to stand up. Hand out a number card to each person in the group in sequence (the even numbers are printed in a different colour). Say that you are going to count in twos then point to everyone but *say* only the even numbers (e.g. point silently/point and say two/point silently/point and say four).

Say that the numbers two, four, six and eight are called even numbers.

The numbers one, three, five, seven and nine are called odd numbers.

Encourage the group to do this themselves by asking only the person holding an even number card to say their number. Go round several times.

Then ask the group to tell you which numbers you *didn't* say. Ask the even numbers to sit down, then read out the odd numbers and say that the even numbers are sitting down so that those standing up have **odd numbers**.

Next, play the odd and even number game where you call out a series of activities which you want the odd or even number holders to do, e.g.:

- Odd numbers stand up.
- Even numbers turn around.
- Odd numbers touch your ears.

Half and half

(Sitting)

Lay out eight objects. Two animals have to have half each. The children help them to work this out.

use
pondering
take your
time

Closing round – Same as me, different from me

(Standing)

Ask the group to look at you while you hold up three fingers. Say the name of someone in the group and ask them to hold up the same fingers as you and then to tell you how many fingers they are holding up. They then have to hold up their fingers and ask someone else to count them (e.g. *'Kuli – how many fingers am I holding up?'*). Kuli replies with the correct number, then he holds up (e.g. four fingers) and asks Peter: *'Peter – how many fingers am I holding up?'*

Then instead of asking the children to do the same as you, tell them they must do something different:

- So that when you hold up three fingers they must hold up a different number.

    Emphasise the word **different**.

Session 25

Materials

- Three cubes for each person in the group plus one extra.
- Toy bear.
- Yellow hoops.
- Large cloth.
- Red and blue square and triangle shapes to share around the group.
- Three toy animals.
- Objects in a jar.
- Addy the Adder (a little snake puppet with a plus sign on her back).
- Sid the Subtractor (a little snake puppet with a minus sign on his back).

Many numbers

(Standing, then sitting)

Give a number verbally to each person in the group, then as you call out the number they sit down.

Have you enough for Mr Bear?

(Sitting)

Give each person in the group two cubes but give one person an extra one so that they have three cubes.

Introduce Mr Bear who will ask them to help him by giving him the number of cubes that he asks for.

Mr Bear then asks each person around the circle: *'Can you give me three cubes? Have you enough?'*

Each person tells Mr Bear how many cubes they have and whether they have enough to give him three. Then the person who has three cubes changes places with Mr Bear. Mr Bear gives them their cubes back: *'Mr Bear wants everyone to have **one more**'.*

He ponders lightly and briefly: *'How many will you each have then?'*

Ask the children for their thoughts and ideas.

Mr Bear then gives one more cube to each person saying, *'Here is one more. If I give you this how many will you have?'*

When everyone in the group has their cubes back he asks: *'Can you give me four cubes? Have you enough?'*

Only the person who had three cubes last time will have enough, so they change places with Mr Bear again.

Ponder why that is and talk about three and **one more** being four. The rest of the group all have **one less**, so they have three.

Mr Bear thanks the group and is put away.

Making up groups

(Standing)

Put out two yellow hoops. Hand out the red and blue shapes. Invite the children to form two groups standing in the hoops. Ask the children to give you ideas about what groups you could make (e.g. a red group and a blue group). Recall what pattern you made last time.

When the children have identified these two groups bring them back into the circle again and ask if there are any other ways they could make two groups (i.e. squares and triangles).

Tell me one more

(Sitting)

Put the three toy animals in the middle of the circle with an object in front of each of them. Invite children individually to take one object from your jar and to tell you which animal they will give 'one more' to and how many that animal will have then.

Frequently use the term 'one more', commenting, *'Two is one more than one'* and *'Three is one more than two'* and so on. At the end of this game, collect the objects and see if the children can tell you what one more than a given number is. Do this, for example, by putting down two objects and saying, *'If you add one more how many will there be?'*

**use
pondering
take your
time**

Addy the Adder and Sid the Subtractor

(Standing)

The children sit in a circle with a large cloth in the middle. Reintroduce Addy the Adder.

Addy then chooses people in the group, one by one, to stand on the cloth in the middle of the circle. Each time Addy says, *'I'm going to add one more person'*, and chooses one person from the group to join the person(s) in the middle. Ask the group each time to say how many people there are in the middle now.

When everyone apart from you is in the middle, Addy the Adder says she is going to go to the shops but she will be back next week.

Say that you want to see how many people are in the group. Ask them to stand in a line and count them.

Introduce another snake called Sid the Subtractor. Explain that he takes objects away. Play the game as before but take one person away from the group in the middle to sit back in the circle each time.

Closing round – Time to sing

(Sitting, then standing)

Talk to the group about what they did this morning when they got to school. Select five of these activities and put them into a little chant as follows:

> This morning I walked to school,
> This morning I had my break,
> This morning I looked at a book,
> This morning I played,
> and then I drew a picture.

Chorus:

> That's what we do in the morning.

Stand up with the group and sing this together.

Session 26

Materials
- Addy the Adder (a little snake puppet with a plus sign on her back).
- Sid the Subtractor (a little snake puppet with a minus sign on his back).
- Large cloth.

Time to sing

(Sitting, then standing)

Talk to the group about what they did this morning **before** they came to school. Then talk about what they did later in the morning **after** they get to school. Select four or five more of these activities and put them into a little chant as follows:

> This morning I had play time,
> This morning I did some drawing,
> And then I did some number work.

Chorus:

> That's what we do after we come to school
> in the morning.

relax and have fun

Note that you may have to be a bit flexible with the way this scans!

Stand up with the group and sing this together.

Addy the Adder and Sid the Subtractor

(Standing)

The children sit in a circle with a large cloth in the middle. Reintroduce Addy the Adder and Sid the Subtractor.

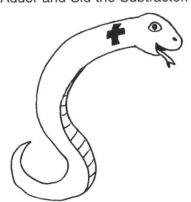

Addy then chooses people in the group, one by one, to stand on the cloth in the middle of the circle. Each time Addy says, *'I'm going to add one more person'*, and chooses one person from the group to join the person(s) in the middle. Ask the group each time to say how many people there are in the middle now.

When everyone apart from you is in the middle, Addy the Adder says she is going to hide and see if Sid the Subtractor takes away the people in the middle.

Make a little drama of Sid saying, *'Ha ha, Addy has added all these people together. I'm going to take some away.'*

Sid goes around the group considering, then he chooses one person to take away each time to sit back in the circle. Altogether he takes away all but one of the people.

Addy the Adder comes in crossly and says, *'Ha Ha! I thought it was you taking people away when I had added them altogether'*, and she adds two more people. Ask the children how many there are in the group now you have **added** two more.

Create a little scenario where Sid takes people away and Addy adds them back again. Introduce the question each time and ponder, *'Are there more or less (fewer) now?'*

Closing round – Different shape names

(Sitting)

Explain that each person will say a shape name but it must be different from the person just before him or her. Demonstrate: *'If I say square you say a different shape name.'*

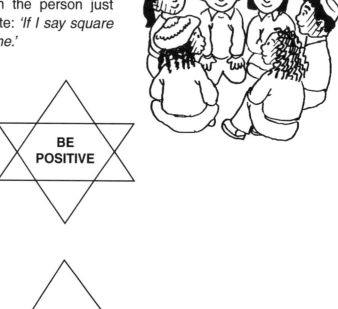

BE POSITIVE

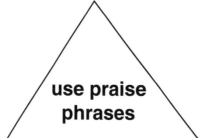

use praise phrases

Session 27

Materials
- Number card for each person in the group.
- Two toys (one has a badge with one object on, the other has a badge with two objects on to represent odd and even). You could make them different colours if you wish.
- Hedgehog and King puppets.
- Three cloth shapes – triangular, square and circular.
- Assorted wooden or plastic shapes.
- Circles – one for each person (red and blue).

Counting in twos

(Standing)

Hand out a number card to each person in the group in sequence. Say that you are going to count in twos, then point to everyone but only *say* the even numbers (e.g. point silently/point and say two/point silently/point and say four). Remind the children why they are called odd and even numbers.

Encourage the children to do this themselves by asking only the person holding an even number card to say their number. Go around the group several times.

Then ask the group to tell you which numbers you *didn't* say. Ask the even numbers to sit down, then read out the odd numbers and say that the even numbers are sitting down so that those standing up have **odd numbers**.

Next, play the odd and even number game where you call out a series of activities which you want the odd or even number holders to do, for example:

- Odd numbers stand up.
- Even numbers turn around.
- Odd number touch your ears.

Hold on to the cards for the next game.

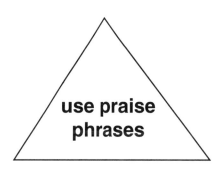

use praise phrases

The odd and even number toys

(Standing)

Explain that the toys are wearing badges with either one or two stars to represent odd and even. The one with one star on it collects odd numbers and the other with two stars on it collects even numbers. Choose two people to carry the two toys.

Help the 'even' toy to collect people with even numbers for his line, then help the 'odd' toy to collect the odd number people. Then let the toys have turns to take the group for a jump/skip/hop around the room.

Time to sing

(Sitting, then standing)

Talk to the children about what they did at lunch-time. Select a few of these activities and put them into a chant as follows:

> At lunch-time I heard the bell,
> At lunch-time I ate my sandwiches,
> At lunch-time I went out to play,
> That's what I do at lunch-time.

relax and
have fun

Hedgehog's shape treasure hunt

(Sitting)

Tell the children that you are going to be helping the King to hide some shapes so that the hedgehog can have a treasure hunt, which means that he will collect as many shapes as he can.

Lay out in the middle of the circle the three cloths – triangular, circular and square. Ask the King to choose individual children to show him a wooden shape and say that if they can tell you what shape it is, they can tell you which cloth to hide it under.

Encourage the children to tell you which cloth they want you to hide the shape under. It is important at this point to encourage use of the language.

The children then tell the King which cloth they would like the shape hidden under.

When all the shapes are hidden bring in the hedgehog. He is quite excited about playing the game. He says, *'I would like to find a nice circle. Can you give me clues so that I will know where to look?'*

The King asks, *'What types of clue would you like?'*

The hedgehog replies: *'Well if you would say things like the circle treasure is under a cloth with three sides and three corners then I will know that I will need to look under the triangle cloth.'*

Help the hedgehog to find the shapes he chooses by describing the properties of the cloth each shape is hidden under.

use pondering take your time

Closing round – Patterns

(Sitting in a semicircle to leave a space for children to line up; lay out the previous pattern of triangles and circles made by the group)

Place circles and triangles in a group on the floor in front of you. Ask one child to choose a colour and to stand up in the space in the circle.

Ask another child to choose a colour and stand next to the first child. Talk about the pattern they are making. Ask what shape is next. Talk again about the pattern. Ask each child what shape will be next. Ask the next child to choose that shape and to stand in the line in the right place. Encourage the children to complete a pattern.

Go back into a circle and do a round with each child saying the name of their colour out loud. Cover up the pattern. Sit the children back in the circle. See if the children can remember the pattern.

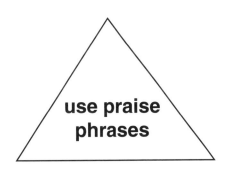

use praise phrases

Session 28

> ## Materials
> - Interesting box containing numbers two and five.
> - Robot mask.
> - Large piece of paper and pen.
> - Spotted dice and small objects which may be put on the dice to cover the spots.

Number box two and five

(Sitting)

Take the numbers out of an interesting box one at a time and pass them around the group. Encourage the children to run their fingers around the numerals' shapes and say 'two' then 'five'. Adults model this as well. Emphasise the need to start at the top of the number. In pairs, draw one of these numbers on a partner's back. He/she has to say which number it is.

The odd and even number toys

(Standing)

Explain that the toys are wearing badges with either one or two stars to represent odd and even. The one with the star on it collects odd numbers and the other with two stars on it collects even numbers. Choose two people to carry the two toys.
Help the 'even' toy to collect people with even numbers for his line, then help the 'odd' toy to collect the odd number people. Then let the toys have turns to take the group for a jump/skip/hop around the room.

Roll the spotted dice with corresponding objects

(Sitting, using eyes not fingers)

Throw the dice. Count the spots on the face of the dice by *looking*, not touching. Choose small objects to correspond with the number of spots. Then place these objects on the spots one by one.

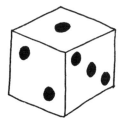

Adult – choose one too many when it is your turn. Talk about *'One too many'*; *'Take away one'*; *'One less'*; *'Correct number'*.

Finally, see if children can recall how many spots each person had.

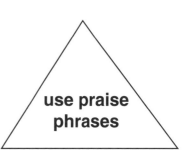

use praise
phrases

Make the robot move

(Sitting)

Select a child to wear a robot mask and be the robot. You can tell the child to move around a square piece of material which you put down in the middle of the circle when told forward, backward or sideways.

Ask the robot to stand in the middle of the square, then to move:

- Forward to a side,
- Backward to the middle,
- Sideways to a side,
- Sideways across to another side,
- Forward to an edge,
- Sideways to an edge,
- Diagonally across the square.

Choose other children to play the part of the robot.

Time to sing

(Sitting, then standing)

Recap on the activities you have talked about in the morning, mid-morning and lunch-time in past sessions. Now talk about things we do in the afternoon and put it into a similar chant, for example:

> In the afternoon we came to class,
> In the afternoon we did some more work,
> We listened to a story,
> And later on we go home
> And have our tea, that's what we do in the afternoon.

Closing round – Two or five?

(Sitting)

Sit with a piece of paper in front of you and draw a two or a five very slowly. The game is for the children to guess which one you are drawing. They then have to put one finger on their lips to stop them shouting out their guess. With their other hand they also have to hold up the number of fingers to show what number they think it is (make sure you draw with the children behind you so that they 'see' the figure the right way round).

Tell the children they are allowed to change their minds if they think they need to but they must not shout out their answers. Do this several times.

Session 29

Materials

- Three cloths – triangular, circular and square.
- Wooden or plastic shapes – triangular, circular and square.
- Large cloth.
- Addy the Adder and Sid the Subtractor puppets.
- Number cards.

Growing Numbers

(Active)

All crouch on the floor.

Count 'one, two, three, four, and five' as you all get taller. Then stretch your arms right up when you get to five. All clap hands and jump once.

relax and have fun

Circle train with numbers

(Standing)

Randomly assign number cards (one to eight or number in the group) to people in the circle. Choose someone to be the engine. The task for the engine is to sort the carriages in order of number before the train can chug around the room. Ponder and ask, *'Who is first in the line? Who is next? Who is last?'* to the tune of *Here We Go Round the Mulberry Bush.*

> Linda is the first in line, first in line, first in line
> Linda is the first in line on our train.
> David is the last in line, last in line, last in line,
> David is the last in line on our train

Addy the Adder and Sid the Subtractor

(Sitting)

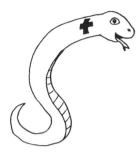

The children sit in a circle with a large cloth in the middle. Re-introduce Addy the Adder and Sid the Subtractor.

This time play a short game with Addy and Sid adding or taking away people from the middle of the group. Then make Addy and Sid appear to whisper to you that they want to play with the children and give them a turn. Choose two children to hold Addy and Sid, and encourage them to play the game.

Encourage use of language and grasp of concept by asking the children whether they will add one more or take away one more before they stand up to play the game.

Number of sides

(Sitting)

Lay out triangle, square and circle shapes in the circle. Place the number cards one to four in the circle. The task for the children is to identify the correct number of sides in each shape and to lay the correct number card on top of that shape (e.g. the triangle would be three, the circle one, and the square and the rectangle four).

Closing round – Time to sing

(Sitting, then standing)

Recap on the activities you have talked about in the morning, mid-morning, lunchtime and afternoon in past sessions. Now talk about things we do in the evening and put them into a similar chant, for example:

> In the evening we are at home,
> In the evening we watch some TV,
> In the evening we play,
> In the evening we have a bath,
> And later we go to bed,
> That's what we do in the evening.

relax and
have fun

Session 30

```
┌─────────────────────────────────────────────────────────┐
│                      Materials                           │
│  • Robot mask.                                           │
│  • Square piece of material.                             │
│  • Tambourine.                                           │
│  • Felt-tip pen and A3 sheet of paper.                   │
└─────────────────────────────────────────────────────────┘
```

Do the same and different to me

(Standing)

Ask the children to do the same as you:

- Touch your nose.
- Put your hands behind your back.
- Hop… and so on.

Choose one of the children to be the leader.

Ask the children to do different things from you:

- Touch your nose
- Put your hands behind your back
- Hop… and so on

Choose one of the children to be the leader.

Make the robot move

(Sitting)

Select a child to wear a robot mask and be the robot. You can tell them to move around a square piece of material – which you put down in the middle of the circle – when told: forward, backward, or sideways.

Ask the robot to stand in the middle of the square and then do a selection of these moves:

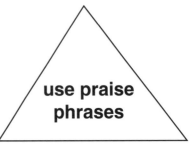

- Forward to a side,
- Backward to the middle,
- Sideways to a side,
- Sideways across to another side,
- Forward to an edge,
- Sideways to an edge,
- Diagonally across the square.

Choose other children to direct the robot. Check with them that the robot has done what they wanted it to do.

Same as the tambourine beats

(Standing)

The children move in a circle to the beat of the tambourine.
Say that they must stand still and listen and count the beats
of the tambourine, then to take that many steps. Talk about
leaving enough space and which foot to start off with in
order to go around co-ordinated as a group.

Three or four?

(Sitting)

Sit with a piece of paper in front of you and begin to draw
a three or a four very slowly. The game is for the children
to guess which one you are drawing. They then have to
put one finger on their lips to stop them shouting out their
guess. Using their other hand they also have to hold up
the number of fingers to show what number they think it
is.

use
pondering
take your
time

    Tell the children that they are allowed to change their
mind if they think they need to but they must not shout
out their answers. Do this several times.

Closing round – Time to sing: night-time

(Sitting then standing)

Recap on the activities you have talked about in the morning, mid-morning, lunch-
time, afternoon and evening in past sessions. Now talk about things we do at night-
time and put it into a similar chant, for example:

> At night-time we brush our teeth,
> At night-time we go to bed,
> At night-time we see the moon,
> At night-time we go to sleep,
> That's what we do at night-time.

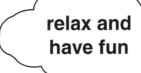

relax and
have fun

97

Session 31

Materials
- Squares and triangles in a basket.
- Zebra and bear or two other animals.
- Cards one to ten (one per person in the group).
- Two toys with a one- or two-star badge.

The shape basket game

(Sitting and standing, using only squares and triangles, using two colours)

Prepare first by identifying how many sides and how many corners each shape has.

Play by alternating instructions of:

- Triangles – hop on one leg.
- Squares – turn around.

Then choose by the number of sides:

- Shapes with three sides – sit down.
- Shapes with four sides – touch your nose and so on.

Now stimulate use of the vocabulary by encouraging the children to give the instructions (e.g. *'Circles change places'*).

> **use
> pondering
> take your
> time**

Zebra and bear share

(Sitting)

Bring in two animals to 'help' put the shapes away. Give each unequal amounts, then role-play the zebra (e.g. saying, *'You have more than me, that's not fair. We should have the same!'*).

The other animal agrees and gives the zebra most of their shapes. Then after a pause the other animal says, *'Wait; now you have more than me, that's not fair! That's not equal, that's unequal!'*

Ask for ideas as to how to make it fair. At the end of the game pass the animals around for children to stroke.

Counting in twos

(Standing)

Give the children a number to remember from one to ten in random order. Ask them to get into a line in order of their number, then give numbers two, four, six and eight a number card. Say, *'I am going to count in twos and when you hear your number you must sit down.'*

Point to everyone in the line but *say* only the even numbers. Point silently, point and say two, point silently, point and say four and so on.

Next, encourage the group to take an active role. The people holding even number cards say their number out loud. Go around the group several times.

Ask the group to tell you which numbers you didn't say, then bring out the odd number cards and check with the group.

The odd and even number toys

(Standing)

Explain that the toys are wearing badges with either one or two stars to represent odd and even. The one with one star on it collects odd numbers and the other with two stars on it collects even numbers. Choose two people to carry the two toys.

Help the 'even' toy to collect people with even numbers for his line, then help the 'odd' toy to collect the odd number people. Then let the toys have turns to take the group for a jump/skip/hop around the room.

Growing numbers

(Active)

All crouch on the floor. Count, *'One, two, three, four, and five'*, as you all get taller. Then stretch your arms right up when you get to five. All clap hands and jump once.

Closing round – We'll all jump together

(Standing)

Stand in a circle. Give instructions to jump/hop forward, backward, towards the middle.

Session 32

Materials

- Mr Bear soft toy.
- Five piles of small objects.
- Weasel puppet (or other).
- One extra soft toy animal.
- Balance scales.

Growing numbers

(Active)

All crouch on the floor. Count, *'One, two, three, four, and five'*, as you all get taller. Then stretch your arms right up when you get to five. All clap hands and jump once.

Mr Bear's missing number game

(Sitting)

Mr Bear puts out piles of objects from one to five. He counts and emphasises that they are in number order. He asks the children to watch them for him and goes behind the adult's back.

Enter the mischievous weasel who looks at the piles of objects, chooses pile four, takes away the objects and hides them under the box. He then moves the remaining piles of objects to change their order.

Mr Bear comes back and notices that one pile of objects is missing. Mr Weasel says that he will give the things back if Mr Bear can guess which pile is missing, but warns that if he gets it wrong he won't!

Mr Bear asks the children if he knows which pile it is and how he can check how many objects were in that pile.

With the group problem-solve ways to check this by putting the piles back in number order and seeing which pile is missing. Encourage strategies such as choosing one person to represent each number one to five; or getting them to line up in order then retrieve their pile of objects.

When the correct pile is identified the mischievous weasel gives the pile back.

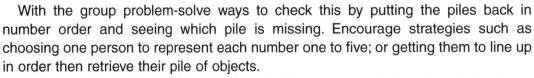

**use
pondering
take your
time**

Lightest, heaviest

(Sitting)

Three animals argue about which is the lightest and which is the heaviest. The group helps them to work this out. Talk about checking this using balance scales. Explain the effects that a heavier weight will have (e.g. a heavier weight will bring that side of the scales down).

Closing round – Different shape names

(Sitting)

Explain that each person will say a shape name but it must be different from the person just before him or her. Demonstrate: *'So if I say square you cannot say square but you could say triangle. You mustn't say square. If you say triangle the next person cannot say triangle but could say circle or square.'*

Session 33

Materials
- Large piece of paper.
- Dotted counting cards.
- Spotty dog mark.
- Weasel puppet.
- Lion cub puppet.
- Two badges with either one star or two stars.
- Three squares of cardboard.

Long steps, short steps

(Standing)

Discuss with the children what is a short step and what is a long step. Then take turns to call out long step or short step for the children to copy. Get each child to take a turn.

Three, five or eight?

(Sitting)

Sit with a piece of paper in front of you and begin to draw a three, five or eight very slowly. The game is for the children to guess which one you are drawing. They also have to hold up the number of fingers to show what number they think it is.

Tell the children they are allowed to change their minds if they think they need to but they must not shout out their answers. Do this several times.

**use
pondering
take your
time**

Ice-creams for everyone

(Sitting. Use coloured counters as biscuits if ice-creams are not available)

Pass around a box containing lots of small toy animals and ask everyone to take out a handful. Then use the pictures of the ice-creams cut out from the Appendix. Tell a story of the ice-cream man who comes into the woods to sell ice-creams to the animals. Say, *'I've got three animals. I will need three ice-creams'* and take three ice-creams.

Ask each person in the circle *'How many animals have you got?'* and, *'How many ice-creams will you need?'*

Encourage the children to choose the number of ice-creams corresponding to what they say. This will help with checking one-to-one correspondence and use of language for number.

Spotty dog

(Standing)

One of the adults holds the spotty dog picture and dog without spots. The dog has to collect his spots. He needs to collect one spot first then his spots from the head down towards the tail. Ask, *'Who has got one spot? Come and hold the picture of the spotty dog. Who has got two spots? . . . come and stand behind . . .'* and so on, making a line to represent the spotty dog. Encourage the children to identify this by themselves. Children with more spots are at the 'tail end' – as in the picture.

When *everyone* is in the line:

Ask which person is **first** and which person **last** – who has a few spots – as the front/head of the dog, who has more spots – as the tail end of the dog.

Then act out a little story together of the dog sniffing through the grass wagging his tail (hands behind their backs). He yawns and stretches, and curls up to have a sleep.

Little lion cub goes to sleep

(Sitting)

Place on the floor three squares of cardboard; the one in the middle should be dark to represent night-time. The three squares represent day one, night-time and day two. Place the lion cub on the first square to tell the story about being a little cub liking to play games with his friends. He pretends he is asleep while they say, *'Little lion cub, are you awake?'* Just when they have given up he jumps up and says *'boo'* to make them jump. Role-play this with the children.

Next say that the lion cub's mummy told him it was night-time and he had to go to sleep. He curls up on the dark square. The next day (put him on the next square) he thinks out loud: *'I want to play that game again, it was really good but I can't remember it. What did I do again before I went to sleep?'*

Physically put him back on the day one square where he recalls the game he played, then put him back on the day two square where he says, *'Ah yes. I can remember what I played yesterday. I will play it again today.'*

Repeat the re-enactment with the children.

Closing round – Long steps, longer steps

(Standing)

Ask the children to stand in a line. Ask one child to take one small step. Put a marker down. Then go back to the beginning and ask each child in turn to take a longer step.

relax and have fun

Session 34

Materials

- Tambourine.
- Robot mask.
- Large square of material.
- Masks.
- Addy the Adder and Sid the Subtractor (two little sock puppets plus and minus).
- Lion cub puppet.
- Five squares of cardboard, three should be dark.
- Three toy frogs.

Number hops

(Standing)

Pass around the tambourine for everyone to shake. Then say that you will beat the tambourine one, two or three times and call out an action (e.g. when you give one beat say, *'Altogether one hop'* and everyone does one hop, when you say *'Two hops'* everyone does two hops. Then change to *'One jump'* and everyone does one jump, when you say *'Two jumps'* everyone does two jumps and so on around the circle). Then choose individuals by name (e.g. *'Sue can you do three hops?'*).

Addy the Adder and Sid the Subtractor

(Standing)

The children sit in a circle with a large cloth in the middle. Reintroduce Addy the Adder and Sid the Subtractor.

This time play a short game with Addy and Sid, adding or taking away people from the middle of the group. Then make Addy and Sid appear to whisper to you that they want to play with the children and give them a turn. Choose two children to hold Addy and Sid and encourage them to play the game.

Encourage use of language and grasp of concept by asking the children whether they will add one more or take away one more before they stand up to play the game.

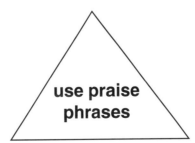

use praise phrases

Make the robot move

(Sitting. Introducing left and right to the instructions)

Select a child to wear a robot mask and be the robot. You can tell the child to move around a square piece of material – which you put down in the middle of the circle – when told: forward, backward or sideways. Remind the children that if they hold their left hand out with their thumb extended it will make an 'L' for left.

Ask the robot to stand in the middle of the square, then perform a selection of these moves:

- Forward to a side.
- Back to the right.
- Left to a side.
- Sideways across to another side.
- Forward to an edge.
- Backward to the right.
- Right to an edge.
- Diagonally across the square.

Choose other children to direct the robot. Check with them that the robot has done what they wanted it to do.

use pondering take your time

Little cub goes to sleep

(Sitting)

Place on the floor five squares of cardboard; every other one should be dark to represent night-time. The five squares represent day one, night-time, day two, night-time and day three.

Place the cub on the first square to tell the story about being a little cub who likes to play games with his friends. He pretends he is asleep while they say, *'Little cub, are you awake?'* Just when they have given up he jumps up and says *'Boo'* to make them jump. Role-play this with the children.

Next say that the cub's mummy told him it was night-time and he had to go to sleep. He curls up on the dark square. The next day (put him on the next square) he thinks out loud: *'I want to play that game again, it was really good, but I can't remember it. What did I do again before I went to sleep?'*

Physically put him back on the day one square where he recalls the game he played. Then put him back on the day two square where he says, *'Ah yes! I can remember what I played yesterday. Hmm, just to make sure I will go back again.'* He rehearses the same game and returns to the day two square where he confidently plays it.

Repeat the re-enactment with the children.

Then at the end of this the cub goes to sleep on the second night-time square. He then wakes up on the day three square. He goes back to the day before to remember, then goes to day three again and so on.

First, second and third

(Sitting)

Choose three children to sit in a row. Give them three frogs, one each. They take turns to make a frog hop as far as they can, then judge which frog is the first, second or third in distance (i.e. the biggest hop).

Closing round – We'll all jump together

(Standing)

Stand in a circle. Give repeat instructions to jump forward, backward, towards the middle.

Session 35

Materials

- Map.
- Badger puppet.
- Toy bear.
- Four frog puppets or toys.
- Shape objects in a feely bag.
- Five plus one cubes for each child in the group.
- Four plastic or toy frogs for each child in the group.

Shape feely bag

(Sitting)

Pass around objects in a feely bag. Each person takes out an object and decides (with the group's help if necessary) what shapes they can see in it. Ask how you can tell it is a certain shape. Help children to talk about sides and corners (e.g. *'How do you know it's a square – yes it has four sides and four corners'*). Slide along the sides and count them. Or *'Yes, it's a circle. It has one long curved edge and no corners.'*

At the end of this game gather in the shapes by saying, *'Can you give me a round blue shape? Can you give me something with straight sides?'* Gather in the objects by describing their attributes. Simplify or extend these instructions in accordance with the needs of the group.

use pondering take your time

Mr Badger's map

(Sitting)

Show the map to the children and talk about what you can see on it. Explain that Mr Badger has lost a nut and they have to guess where it could be. They then have to guide Mr Badger by telling him which roads to go along using the words *'Forward, straight, back, backward, along, beside, round the corner, nearly there, almost there, a little way further'*. Decide yourself when and where the 'nut' will be found.

Have you enough for Mr Bear?

(Sitting)

Give each person in the group four cubes but give one person an extra one so that they have five cubes.

Introduce Mr Bear, who will ask them to help him by giving him the number of cubes that he asks for.

The bear then asks each person around the circle: *'Can you give me five cubes? Have you enough?'*

Each person tells Mr Bear how many cubes they have and whether they have enough to give him five. Then the person who has five cubes gives Mr Bear their cubes and changes places with him. Mr Bear gives them back their cubes: *'Mr Bear wants everyone to have **one more**.'*

He ponders lightly and briefly, *'How many will you each have then?'*

Ask the group for thoughts and ideas.

Mr Bear then gives one more cube to each person, saying, *'Here is one more. If I give you this how many will you have?'*

When everyone in the group has one more cube he asks: *'Can you give me six cubes? Have you enough?'*

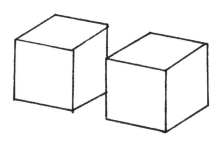

Then only the person who had five cubes last time will have enough, so they change places with Mr Bear again.

Ponder why that is and talk about five and **one more** being six. The rest of the group all have **one less**, so they have five.

Mr Bear thanks the group and wonders aloud: *'How many cubes there are **altogether**?'* He suggests that all the cubes are put in the middle of the circle and that the children help him to count how many there are. The cubes are then put away.

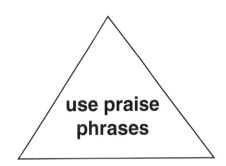

use pondering take your time

use praise phrases

First, second and third

(Sitting)

Choose four children to sit in a row. Give them a frog each. They take turns to make the frog hop as far as they can, then judge which frog is the first, second, third or fourth in distance (i.e. the biggest hop).

relax and have fun

Closing round – Don't do the same as me

(Standing)

Instead of asking the children to do the same as you, tell them they must do something different:

- So that when you touch your nose they must perform a different action.
- Put your hands behind your back.
- Hop . . . and so on.

Emphasise the word **different**.

  Choose one of the children to be the leader to continue the game.

Session 36

Materials
- Map.
- Badger puppet.
- Jar containing small animals (plastic or paper).

We'll all jump together

(Standing)

Stand in a circle. Give instructions to jump forward, backward, towards the middle.

Mr Badger's map

(Sitting)

Show the map to the children and talk about what you can see on it. Explain that Mr Badger has lost a nut and they have to guess where it could be. They then have to guide Mr Badger by telling him which roads to go along using the words *'Forward, back, backward, right, left along, beside, round the corner, almost there, a little way further'*. Decide yourself when and where the 'nut' will be found.

Rows and circles

(Standing)

Tell the children that you would like them to line up in a row. Then ask them to form a circle. Then ask them to form a row again. Give help where needed to achieve this. Ask the children to form two rows. Encourage line-up neatly with one-to-one correspondence.

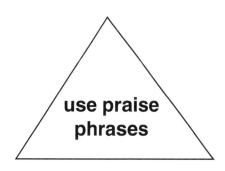

use praise phrases

Ice-creams for everyone

(Sitting. Use coloured counters as biscuits if ice-creams are not available)

Pass around the jar containing lots of small toy animals and ask everyone to take out a handful. Then use the pictures of the ice-creams cut out from the Appendix. Tell a story of the ice-cream man who comes into the woods to sell ice-creams to the animals.

Say, *'I've got three animals. I will need three ice-creams'* and take three ice-creams.

Ask each person in the circle, *'How many animals have you got?'* and, *'How many ice-creams will you need?'*

Encourage the children to choose the number of ice-creams corresponding to what they say. This will help with checking one-to-one correspondence and use of language for number.

Circle train with numbers

(Standing)

Randomly assign number cards (one to eight or number in the group) to people in the circle. Choose someone to be the engine. The task for the engine is to sort the carriages in order of number before the train can chug around the room. Ponder and ask, *'Who is first in the line? Who is next? Who is last?'* to the tune of *Here We Go Round the Mulberry Bush.*

> Geoffrey is the first in line, first in line, first in line,
> Geoffrey is the first in line on our train.
> Jenny is the last in line, last in line, last in line,
> Jenny is the last in line on our train.

**use
pondering
take your
time**

Give me another

(Sitting)

Place the jar of small animals in the centre of the circle. Ask a child to give you one animal and then ask another child to give you **another** one. Each time stress, *'Another one, you've given me another one.'*

   At the end say 'No more thank you.'

Closing round – From small to tall

(Standing)

Crouch down and make yourselves as small as you can. Slowly get taller and taller with your arms stretched up high. Leap up and clap your hands and pass a smile around the group.

Appendix: photocopiables

© 2004 Marion Nash and Jackie Lowe *Language Development for Maths*, David Fulton Publishers.

© 2004 Marion Nash and Jackie Lowe *Language Development for Maths*, David Fulton Publishers.

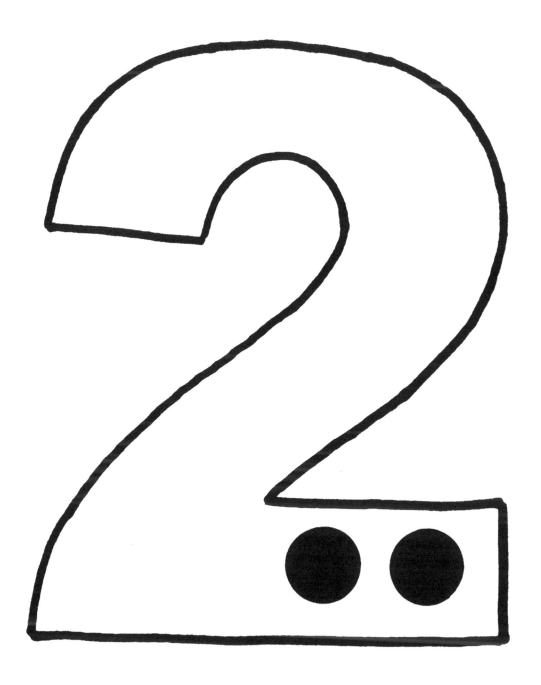

© 2004 Marion Nash and Jackie Lowe *Language Development for Maths*, David Fulton Publishers.

© 2004 Marion Nash and Jackie Lowe *Language Development for Maths*, David Fulton Publishers.

118

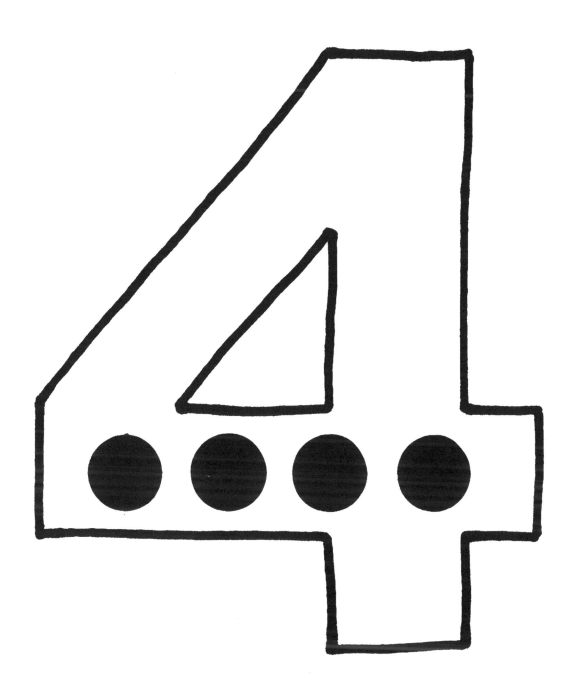

© 2004 Marion Nash and Jackie Lowe *Language Development for Maths*, David Fulton Publishers.

© 2004 Marion Nash and Jackie Lowe *Language Development for Maths*, David Fulton Publishers.

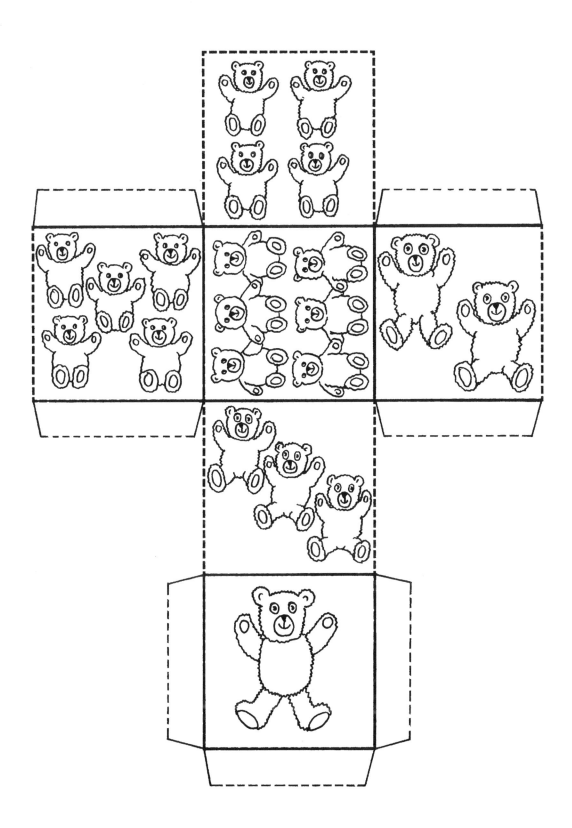

© 2004 Marion Nash and Jackie Lowe *Language Development for Maths*, David Fulton Publishers.

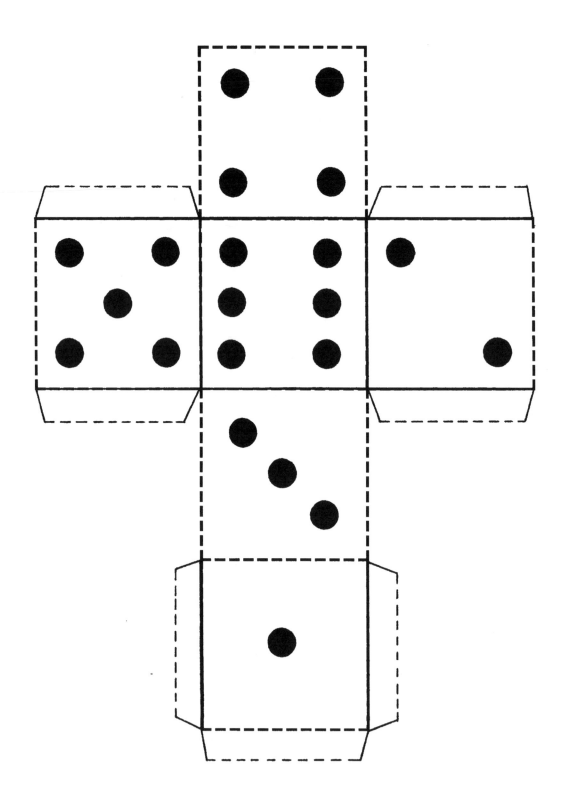

© 2004 Marion Nash and Jackie Lowe *Language Development for Maths*, David Fulton Publishers.

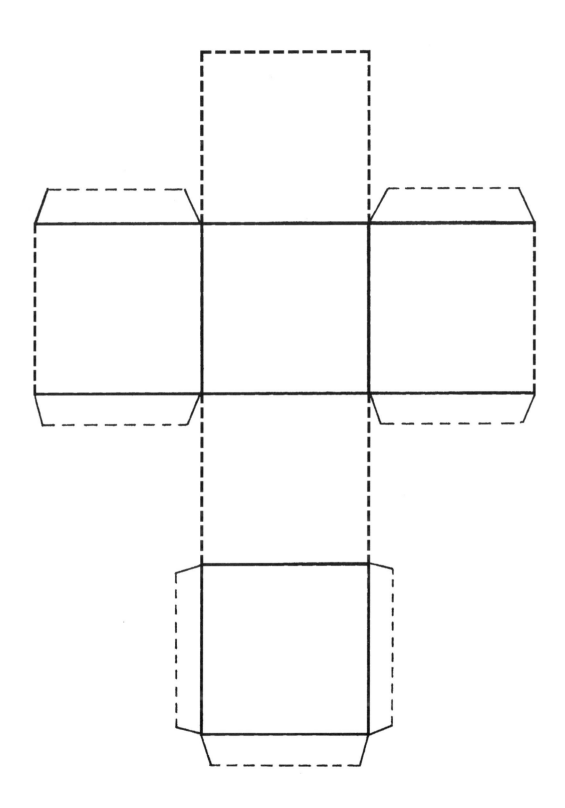

© 2004 Marion Nash and Jackie Lowe *Language Development for Maths*, David Fulton Publishers.

© 2004 Marion Nash and Jackie Lowe *Language Development for Maths*, David Fulton Publishers.

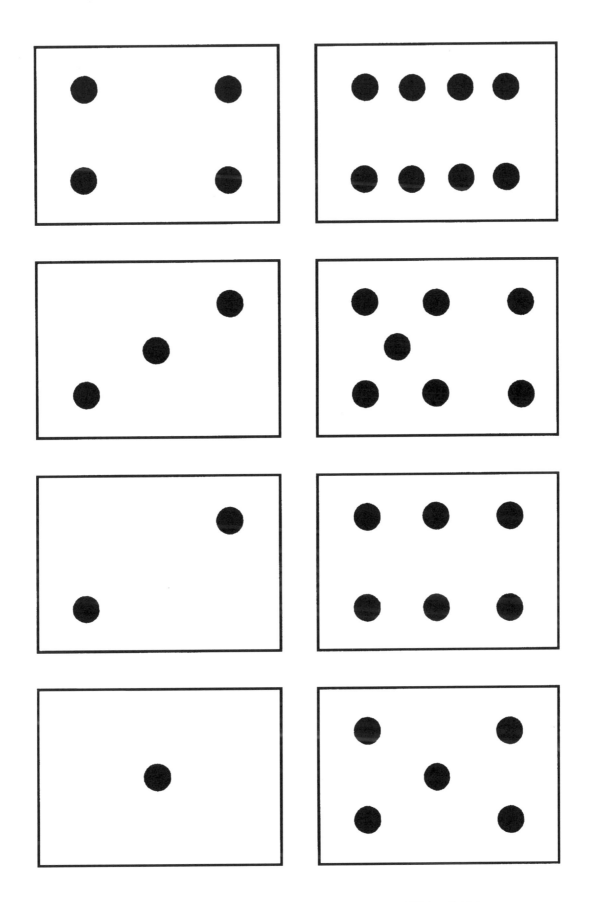

© 2004 Marion Nash and Jackie Lowe *Language Development for Maths*, David Fulton Publishers.

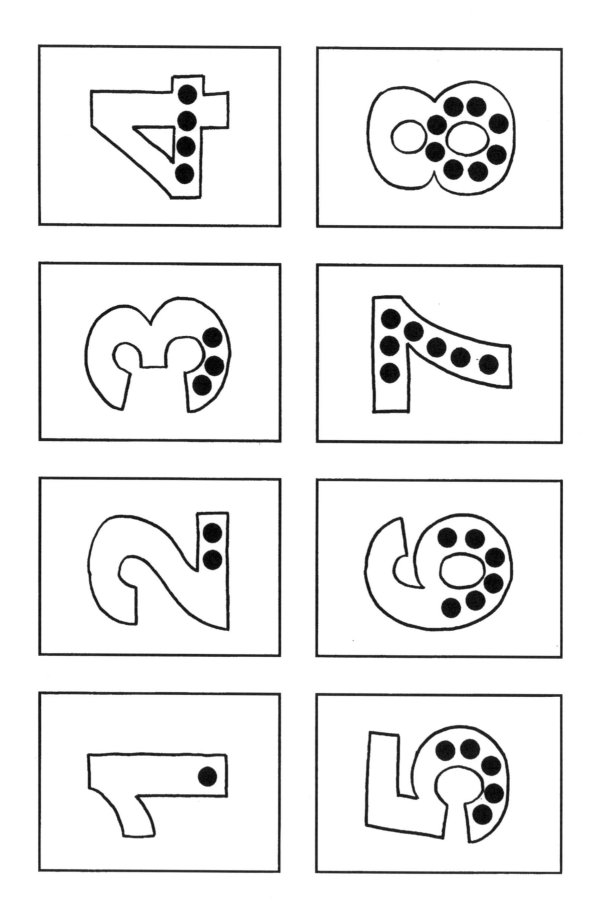

© 2004 Marion Nash and Jackie Lowe *Language Development for Maths*, David Fulton Publishers.

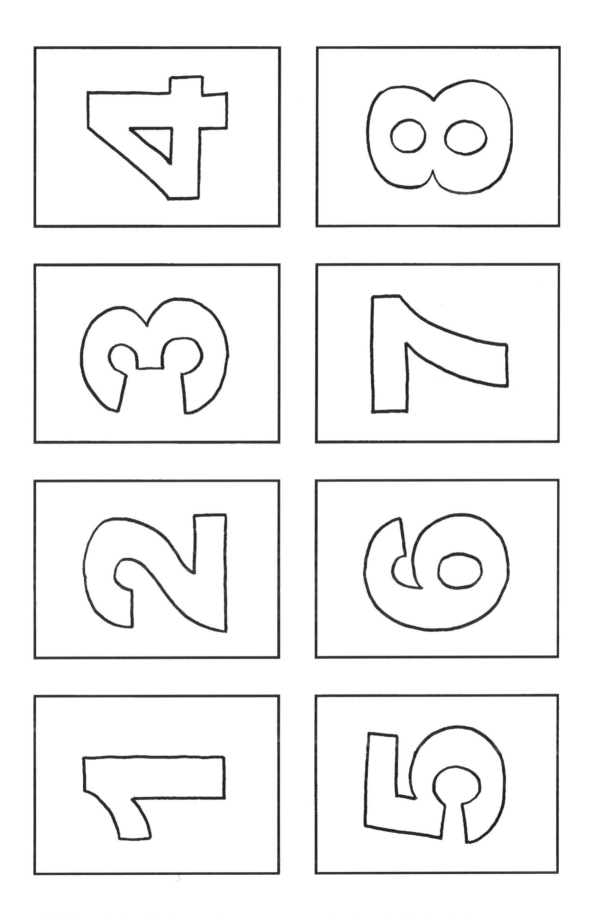

© 2004 Marion Nash and Jackie Lowe *Language Development for Maths*, David Fulton Publishers.

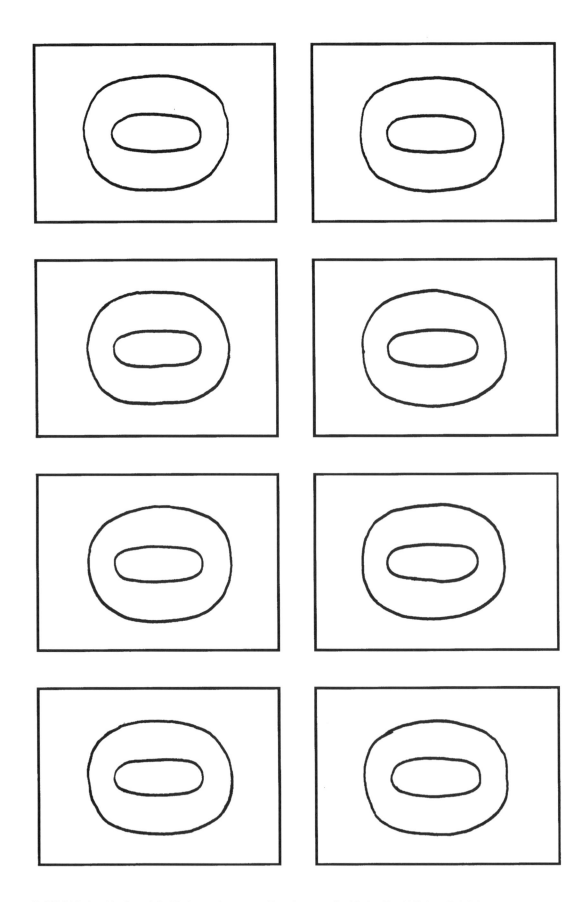

© 2004 Marion Nash and Jackie Lowe *Language Development for Maths*, David Fulton Publishers.

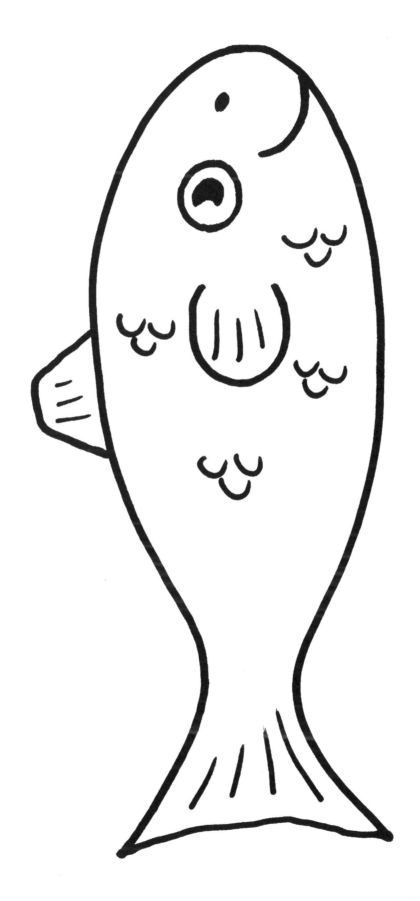

© 2004 Marion Nash and Jackie Lowe *Language Development for Maths*, David Fulton Publishers.

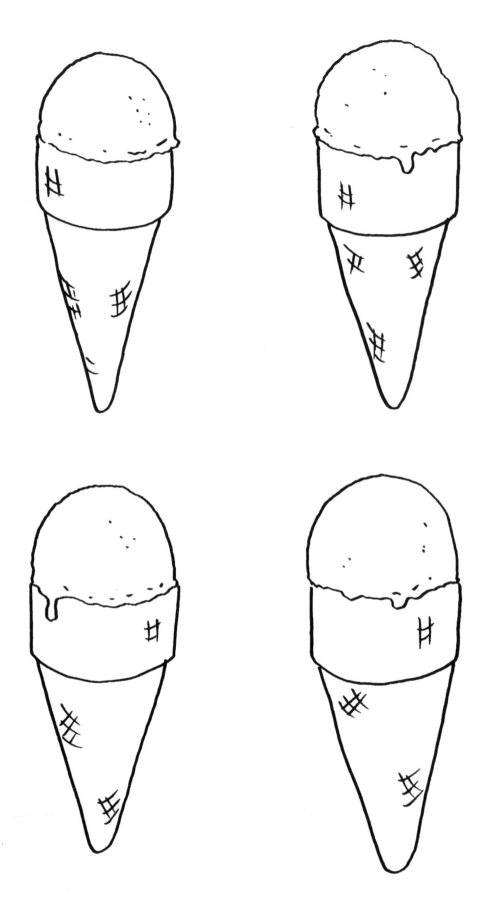

© 2004 Marion Nash and Jackie Lowe *Language Development for Maths*, David Fulton Publishers.

© 2004 Marion Nash and Jackie Lowe *Language Development for Maths*, David Fulton Publishers.

© 2004 Marion Nash and Jackie Lowe *Language Development for Maths*, David Fulton Publishers.

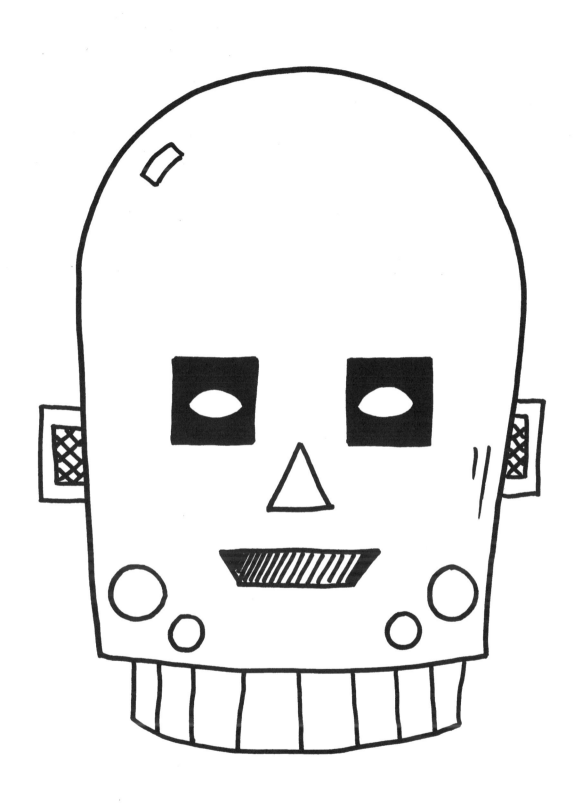

© 2004 Marion Nash and Jackie Lowe *Language Development for Maths*, David Fulton Publishers.

© 2004 Marion Nash and Jackie Lowe *Language Development for Maths*, David Fulton Publishers.

© 2004 Marion Nash and Jackie Lowe *Language Development for Maths*, David Fulton Publishers.

© 2004 Marion Nash and Jackie Lowe *Language Development for Maths*, David Fulton Publishers.

© 2004 Marion Nash and Jackie Lowe *Language Development for Maths*, David Fulton Publishers.

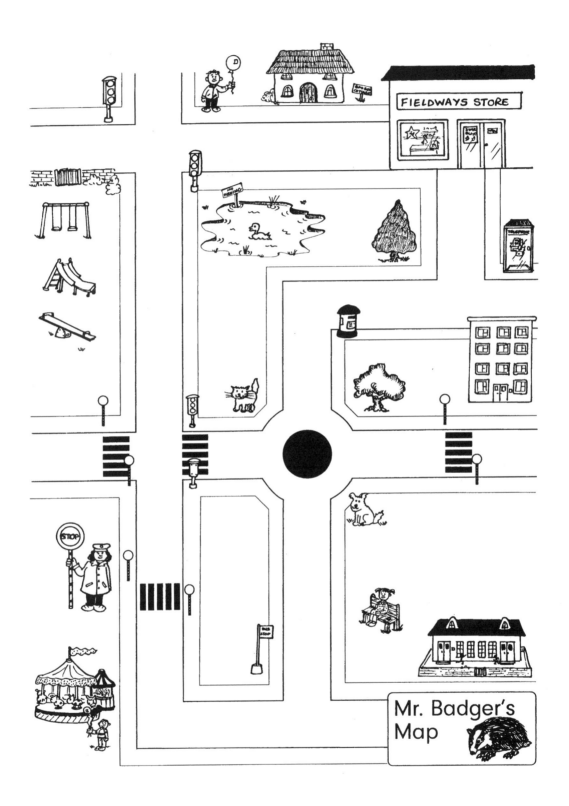

Mr. Badger's Map

© Helen Rippon, Black Sheep Press.

138

Help your children develop their language skills today!

David Fulton Publishers

Spirals This innovative new series addresses young children's language development needs in English, Maths and Science. Based on the spirals programme, developed by Marion Nash and successfully trialled in Plymouth schools, the books link work done in nursery or school with simple play-based activities for the children to do at home.

Ideal for Pre-school, KS1 & KS2

Focusing on English, Maths and Science the series consists of:

A class book that:

- employs a kinaesthetic approach, involving movement, singing, speaking and listening

- contains pre-planned sessions that can run over 2 terms or more

- has an accompanying Video CD providing explanations and demonstrations of the programme and its implementation, with comments from staff who have used it. Ideal for staff training!

An accompanying 'Activities for Home' book which includes:

- simple play-based activities focused on 'learning by doing' that you can photocopy and send home for parents to do with their children and reinforce the school-based sessions. The activities use everyday objects that are found at home and the book includes illustrated prompts to help parents.

> **No other books for language development focus on other core areas of the curriculum. Order yours today!**

Send your order to: David Fulton Publishers, The Chiswick Centre, 414 Chiswick High Road, London W4 5TF
Tel: 0208 996 3610 **Fax:** 0208 996 3622 **Email:** mail@fultonpublishers.co.uk **Website:** www.fultonpublishers.co.uk

English

Language Development
Circle Time Sessions to Improve Communication Skills
£17.00 • 144pp
1-84312-156-5 • 2003

Language Development
Activities for Home
£12.00 • 144pp
1-84312-170-0 • January 2004

OUT NOW!

Maths

Language Development for Maths
Circle Time Sessions to Improve Language Skills
£18.00 • 144pp
1-84312-171-9 • August 2004

Language Development for Maths
Activities for Home
£12.00 • 144pp
1-84312-172-7 • August 2004

Aug 2004!

Science

Language Development for Science
Circle Time Sessions to Improve Language Skills
£18.00 • 144pp
1-84312-173-5 • March 2005

Language Development for Science
Activities for Home
£12.00 • 144 pp
1-84312-174-3 • March 2005

March 2005

Sample activities for school

Sample activities for home

ORDER FORM

Qty	ISBN	Title	Price	Subtotal
	1-84312-156-5	Language Development	£17.00	
	1-84312-170-0	Language Development	£12.00	
	1-84312-171-9	Language Development for Maths	£18.00	
	1-84312-172-7	Language Development Maths	£12.00	
	1-84312-173-5	Language Development for Science	£18.00	
	1-84312-174-3	Language Development Science	£12.00	
			P&P	
			TOTAL	

Free p&p for Schools, LEAs and other Organisations.

Payment

☐ Please invoice
(applicable to schools, LEAs and other institutions)
Invoices will be sent from our distributor, HarperCollins Publishers

☐ I enclose a cheque payable to David Fulton Publishers Ltd
(include postage and packing)

☐ Please charge to my credit card (Visa/MasterCard, American Express, Switch, Delta)

card number ☐☐☐☐ ☐☐☐☐ ☐☐☐☐ ☐☐☐☐ ☐☐☐☐

expiry date ☐☐ ☐☐

(Switch customers only) valid from ☐☐ ☐☐   issue number ☐

Please complete delivery details

Name: ....

Organisation: ....

....

Address: ....

....

....

....

Postcode: ....

Tel: ....

To order

Send to:
David Fulton Publishers, The Chiswick Centre, 414 Chiswick High Road, London W4 5TF

Freephone:
0500 618 052

Fax:
020 8996 3622

06/04 DF315